Lexical structures

Edinburgh Studies in Theoretical Linguistics

Series Editors: Nikolas Gisborne, University of Edinburgh and
Andrew Hippisley, University of Kentucky

Books in the series address the core sub-disciplines of linguistics –
phonology, morphology, syntax, semantics and pragmatics – and their
interfaces, with a particular focus on novel data from various sources
and their challenges to linguistic theorising.

Series Editors
Nikolas Gisborne is Professor of Linguistics at the University of
Edinburgh.

Andrew Hippisley is Professor of Linguistics and Linguistics
Programme Director at the University of Kentucky.

Editorial Board
Umberto Ansaldo, University of Hong Kong
Balthasar Bickel, Universität Zürich
Olivier Bonami, Université Paris-Sorbonne
Heinz Giegerich, University of Edinburgh
Martin Haspelmath, Max Planck Institute for Evolutionary
Anthropology
Jen Hay, University of Canterbury
Stefan Müller, Freie Universität Berlin
Mitsuhiko Ota, University of Edinburgh
Robert Truswell, University of Ottawa
David Willis, University of Cambridge
Alan Yu, University of Chicago

Titles available in the series:

Visit the Edinburgh Studies in Theoretical Linguistics website at
www.euppublishing.com/series/esitl

Lexical structures

Compounding and the modules of grammar

Heinz J. Giegerich

EDINBURGH
University Press

Edinburgh University Press Ltd
The Tun - Holyrood Road
12(2f) Jackson's Entry
Edinburgh EH8 8PJ
www.euppublishing.com

Typeset in 10/12 Sabon by
Servis Filmsetting Ltd, Stockport, Cheshire
and printed and bound in Great Britain by
CPI Group (UK) Ltd, Croydon CR0 4YY

A CIP record for this book is available from the British Library

ISBN 978 0 7486 2461 4 (hardback)
ISBN 978 0 7486 3055 4 (webready PDF)
ISBN 978 1 4744 0815 8 (epub)

Contents

Preamble

This book has two topics. One is the topic of compounding in English, and in particular the long-standing but unresolved research question of the difference between English compound nouns and noun phrases. Is it the case, for example, that *tóy shop* is a compound word and *toy shóp* a phrase, exactly like *dáncing instructor* vs. *dancing instrúctor*? If yes, then what are our criteria for this distinction – especially for the decision to equate *toy shóp* and *dancing instrúctor*? Stress? Semantics? Syntactic behaviour? And if no, then why not? Perhaps because the former is a sequence of two nouns and the latter is not?

The other topic is the theory of lexicalism, with its sub-theory of lexical morphology the only version of generative grammar to have taken a serious interest in the intricacies of words and their structure. It is also the only version to have drawn a sharp modular distinction between the lexicon, where words are formed by the processes of the morphology, and the syntax, where phrases are constructed. This should then be the theory that is best placed to tell the difference between compounds and phrases. But is it?

This engagement with both the empirical and the theoretical gives rise, then, to two questions which of necessity mirror each other: what can compounding in English do for our understanding of the divide between the lexicon and the syntax, and what can lexicalism do for our understanding of the difference between compounds and phrases?

Lexicalism not only posits sharp modular differences but also predicts similarity, in that it expects a given process occurring in one module to have an equivalent process in an adjacent module, distinct from the former only in terms of the characteristics associated with the modules themselves. It is my attention especially to this feature of lexicalism that will constitute a novel approach to the compound–phrase distinction. The distinction between ascriptive and associative attributes, as in *musical child* and *musical director* respectively, developed in Chapter 1, will run through the entire book and figure as the key to our understanding of nominal compounds – of their stress patterns, their syntactic behaviour, their semantics, and of the fact that such compounds normally have 'listed' meaning. But neither this approach nor the theory of lexicalism on which it is based will in the end pin down that elusive compound–phrase distinction. Nor will our findings support the idea, central to lexicalism, of a sharp divide between the two modules of the grammar.

I will argue in the final chapter that not only have we not found these distinctions and divides; they don't actually exist. The modules overlap with each other 'like slates on a roof', and nominal compounding constitutes that overlap, a no-man's land in the grammar which in some respects is neither lexicon nor syntax while in other respects it is both. This result will change the theory of lexicalism almost beyond recognition. Whether it serves to improve the theory or to destroy it is a question for which lexicalists and non-lexicalists will probably offer different answers.

Finally, I need to qualify the term 'novel approach', used above, in two respects.

Firstly, I draw on material here which I have, in one way or another, addressed in previous publications. The lexicon–syntax continuum and its predictions for compounding were sketched in Giegerich (2009a), associative attribution and its implications for compounding in Giegerich (2005a, 2006), the stress criterion in the compound–phrase distinction in Giegerich (2004, 2009b, 2012), and the idea of overlapping modules in Giegerich (2005b). However, bringing these different strands together into a single narrative has prompted significant changes in every one of the individual analyses; and the outcome – that there is no compound–phrase distinction just as there is no lexicon–syntax divide – is not developed anywhere in that earlier work.

Secondly, the term 'novel approach' should not belie the influence others have had, directly or indirectly, on this work. There would be no novel approach here without the work of my students Amira Al-Shehri (on inflection inside compounds), Sarah Anderson, née Collie (on stress preservation effects), Tetsu Koshiishi (on collateral adjectives) and Rebecca Price (on 'Headlinese' compounds). Nor would there be a novel approach without the merciless questioning of the older ones by my Honours and MSc students of English word-formation. I am grateful to all of them, as I am to Laurie Bauer, Nik Gisborne, Dieter Kastovsky†, Rochelle Lieber, Ingo Plag, Geoff Pullum and Graeme Trousdale for many a discussion of these matters, and to EUP and the editors of this series for publishing this book.

Innerleithen, December 2014

Chapter 1

The grammar of adjectival attribution

1.1 Introduction

The single, central theory issue to be addressed in this study is that of the modularisation of the grammar. Is it the case – as is claimed for example in lexicalism (Chomsky 1970) and a long research tradition preceding it, dating back far beyond structuralism – that the grammar is organised into distinct components, including one which handles the morphology (in lexicalism, the lexicon) and another which deals with the syntax? And if so, what is the evidence for such modularisation, and what is the nature of the divide between the two modules? Questions such as those are of interest in their own right for anyone with an interest in how grammar works; for lexicalism, the version of generative grammar notable for a serious interest in morphology and word-formation (Chomsky 1970; Halle 1973; Scalise and Guevara 2005), they are of vital importance.

I propose to explore such questions here by looking at the distinction – purported or real – between noun phrases and compound nouns in English. This is the empirical issue in the focus of this study; and I choose it here for at least two reasons. Firstly, it is an issue which has defied resolution for as long as there has been a discipline of English synchronic linguistics – see, for example, Sweet (1900) for an early statement of the problem. Secondly (and this is why there is an unresolved issue), while English is by no means unique in its ability to concatenate lexemes so as to form not only phrases (*a black bird*) but also complex lexemes (*a blackbird*), the language is unusual for its inability to distinguish the two properly. English compound nouns and noun phrases are not reliably distinct, in terms of inflection, stress or whatever else, as they are for example in German, where a phrase such as *schwarze Drossel* ('black thrush') is easily distinguished from a compound such as *Schwarzdrossel* ('blackbird') on a number of levels. So, in this study we will ask not only what lexicalism can do to illuminate the compound–phrase distinction, but also what that distinction, if it exists, can tell us about the modularisation of the grammar.

The distinction in English between phrase and compound is not necessarily apparent in terms of a single, obvious criterion or a small set of such criteria, as it is in other languages. Moreover, the purported distinction implies the possible presence of a structural ambiguity in the language, such that identical concatenations may qualify for either word or phrase status, and perhaps for both. This fact in particular about English has loomed large in research on English word-formation. Leading Anglists of many generations have attempted (and ultimately failed) to draw a sharp divide between compound and phrase: Sweet (1900), Koziol (1937), Jespersen (1942), Marchand (1969), Faiß (1981), Bauer (1978, 1998), Liberman and Sproat (1992), Olsen (2000, 2001), Bauer et al. (2013) – to name just a few.

There are two possible problems with those attempts. The first is that those researchers (with the notable exceptions of Bauer 1998 and Bauer et al. 2013) have assumed that the divide is present somewhere, waiting to be pinpointed in the data. But perhaps there is no sharp, identifiable divide. Indeed, as we will see, there does not appear to be a single feature shared by all compounds that is not also present in at least some phrases. The widespread failure of the research literature to procure a comprehensive and unique definition of the category 'compound', if indeed there is such a category in English, is due in part to this fuzziness inherent in the criteria (see again Bauer 1998).

But I believe this comparative lack of progress has also been due to a second, methodological problem. By trying to establish a comprehensive taxonomy of compounds, such that there are root compounds, synthetic compounds, *bahuvrihi* compounds, *dvandva* compounds and more, and anything that does not fit into this taxonomy and its criteria is then a phrase, we have simply been focused too closely on the wrong side of the compound–phrase distinction.

I propose therefore, to approach the problem from the opposite direction. Before I turn to compound nouns, I plan first to establish the defining characteristics of their counterparts in the syntax: noun phrases containing pre-modifiers ('attributes'). I choose this different approach not just out of frustration about the failure of the alternative strategy; rather, the new approach is motivated in two rather more positive ways, both of which relate to what we already know about the differences between compound and phrase, or more generally between the lexicon and the syntax as sites for the concatenation of linguistic units.

Firstly, it may be reasonable to assume that entities of the syntax are regular in form, transparent and compositional in meaning, and the outcomes of processes which are fully productive. Entities of the lexicon – morphologically simple and complex words, including compounds – may have these characteristics too but cannot be assumed always to have them. Words too may be the outcomes of productive morphological processes yielding regular form and compositional meaning – perhaps *kindness, pleasantly* and surely certain compounds are examples of those – and may therefore be remarkably similar in nature to entities originating in the syntax. But instead, words may be 'listed' and perhaps fossilised items of irregular form and/or of non-compositional meaning.

Compound nouns, for example, should not be expected to be more regular and uniform than other nouns of the language are (while of course sharing other characteristics with those). Looking for a set of criteria defining what exactly is a compound in English is therefore likely to be misguided. We may be more successful in establishing the characteristics, assumed to be regular and exceptionless, of phrases – in this case, of the type of noun phrase which interfaces with noun compounds: noun phrases containing pre-modifiers ('attributes').

Secondly, and of more immediate importance before we start looking for systematic differences between compounds and phrases, this approach will enable us first to establish the similarities between the two. A tacit recognition of the existence of such similarities clearly lies at the root of the debate about the differences – without it, the need to identify differences would hardly have arisen. But the nature of the similarities has to my knowledge not been spelled out.

Here we may expect to find parallels with findings obtained by the subdiscipline of lexicalism which investigates not the morphology–syntax interface but the interaction of the morphology and syntax with the phonology. The theory distinguishes between 'lexical' and 'postlexical' phonological phenomena, where the former but not the latter interact with the morphology (see for example Mohanan 1986; Giegerich 1999: ch. 4). Typical examples of the lexical phonology are the various consonant alternations found in *electric – electricity – electrician*, or the rules which produce length and height alternations in pairs such as *divine – divinity*. Typical postlexical processes are, for example, those associated with classical allophonies, or those which interact with the syntax (such as phrasal stress).

What is relevant here is that lexical phonological phenomena often have – indeed, are expected to have – phonetically similar postlexical counterparts; and while the two are expected to have different behaviour in certain details, those differences are expected to derive from the more general properties associated with the module in which the process operates. Thus, the palatalisation of alveolar fricatives applies lexically in *race – racial, revise – revision*, where it is obligatory and produces categorical 'phonemic' outputs. Postlexical palatalisation, on the other hand, is optional and produces gradient ('allophonic') outcomes in *miss you, advise you* etc. (Booij and Rubach 1987; McMahon 2000: 50).

The Scottish Vowel Length Rule, governing a categorical long–short distinction among tense vowels in Scottish English and Scots, is a lexical rule (McMahon 2000: 170ff.). It has a postlexical counterpart ('Low-Level Lengthening') affecting all vowels, applying across the board and producing gradient outcomes.

Only lexical rules may be conditioned by features associated with the internal structure of words, such as their morphological structure, or may be associated with specific (sets of) words, or may have random lexical exception. The Scottish Vowel Length Rule exemplifies these character-istics in a particularly striking way. (For details see Giegerich 1992: 229 ff.) In contrast, postlexical processes have no lexical exceptions; and they cannot refer to morphological structure. This 'firewall effect' of the lexicon–postlexicon divide in the phonology is of course also known to hold between the morphology and the syntax, where it is known as 'lexical integrity': this is merely another aspect of the same modular distinction.

So, properties perceived to be associated with individual synchronic phenomena may in reality be properties of the module in which these phenomena occur. This recognition also applies to lexicon-internal modularisation ('stratification'), as we shall see in Chapter 4: the 'conti-nuity of strata hypothesis' (Mohanan 1986: 47). In the present context, it prompts us now to identify the properties of concatenation processes in the lexicon and the syntax respectively, and thus to identify the prin-cipal differences between compounds and phrases. But to do this we must first, encouraged by the parallels seen among lexical and postlexical phonological processes, identify the similarities.

The essential similarity among forms such as *green house* and *green-house*, *wooden bridge* and *stone wall*, *olive oil*, *baby oil* and *engine oil*, and indeed among the two stress variants of *toy factory*, is that they contain nominal, pre-modified heads from which they inherit member-ship of the lexical category Noun. Pre-modifiers in such context ('attrib-utes') may express different things and may, as stress doublets such as *toy fáctory* ('factory which is a toy') – *tóy factory* ('factory which produces toys') demonstrate with particular clarity, enter into different semantic relationships with their heads. I will investigate the nature of attribu-tion in this chapter, without for the moment foregrounding the lexicon–syntax distinction. Later I intend to show that many features of phrasal attribute–head constructions are also found, in similar form, among their lexical ('compound') equivalents. Many of the differences between com-pounds and phrases follow the general pattern of lexical vs. postlexical phenomena familiar on the phonological side from the theory of lexical phonology (Kiparsky 1982; Mohanan 1986; Booij and Rubach 1987; McMahon 2000), as well as being derivative from the even more general properties of the lexicon and the syntax respectively.

1.2 Lexicalism and the syntax–lexicon continuum of attribution

A number of scholars have argued in recent years, many within the theory of construction grammar, a sub-theory of cognitive grammar (Langacker 1987, 1991), that the syntax and the lexicon are not separate modules but that they form some sort of continuum: Croft (2001), Goldberg (2006), Boas (2010), Haspelmath (2011), Broccias (2012) and others. This view is at variance with that of lexicalism, which, as we have seen, posits a sharp dividing line between the two modules. But in lexicalism we also expect a given process to occur in different form on either side of any modular divide: some on contiguous lexical strata (Mohanan 1986; Giegerich 1999), others in both the syntax and the lexicon. Where that leaves the dividing line, and how a modularised grammar can express a continuum, if indeed there is one, is a question to be left until Chapter 5; here we focus on the so-called 'continuum' itself without theorising it.

Let us assume for the moment that the attribute function is typically performed by adjectives. I qualify this assumption in the course of this chapter, distinguishing two kinds of attribution – ascriptive and associative attribution – and arguing that the latter is typically performed by nouns.

English adjectives are held typically to have the following general characteristics, among others. On the syntactic side, they can not only function as attributes to a nominal – *a beautiful picture*, recursively in *a beautiful small picture*; they can also be predicates (*this picture is beautiful*). In both positions they are themselves amenable to pre-modification by degree and other adverbs (*very small, exceptionally beautiful*): most (but as we shall see, not all) adjectives figure as heads of adjective phrases. And they are typically gradable: *smaller, more beautiful* etc.

While these properties (among a few others, irrelevant to the purpose of this chapter – see e.g. Pullum and Huddleston 2002: 527 ff.; Baker 2003: 190 ff.) serve to identify the syntactic behaviour of prototypical adjectives, many specimens of the category fail to display one or perhaps several of those aspects of typical behaviour. Thus, *dental, dead* and *alive* are not gradable; nor will they and a number of others readily permit modification.

Alive moreover cannot occur in the attributive position (**an alive animal*); this and a few other adjectives with the same behaviour contain a historic *a-* prefix (*ablaze, afraid, aghast, alight* etc.; Pullum and Huddleston 2002: 559). Like their prefix (and like the suffix *-en* qualifying *drunk* somewhat archaically for the attribute position: *drunken sailor*), such forms constitute relics from history. Their behaviour is unlikely to be amenable to systematic synchronic explanation.

Other adjectives behave in the opposite way. Thus a specific subclass of adjectives, to be discussed in detail later in this and in the next chapter, cannot occur in the predicate position (*dental decay* – **this decay is dental*); another subclass can have different potential scopes of modification in the two positions. *A beautiful dancer* is ambiguous, as we shall see, but *this dancer is beautiful* is unambiguous. These two subclasses of adjectives have received extensive attention in the literature in the wake of classic treatments by Levi (1978) and Siegel (1980) respectively; unlike their non-attributive counterparts noted above, such adjectives are of significance to the synchronic syntax of English and especially to the compound–phrase distinction at issue here. The former subclass in particular will figure centrally in the argument below, after a brief review of other properties associated with adjectival attribution.

1.2.1 *Intersective vs. subsective attribution*

Adjectival attribution, in its most basic form, is intersective. *Beautiful picture*, for example, denotes a straightforward intersection of a set of pictures and a set of beautiful objects. The set of entities identified by the phrase as a whole is then a proper subset of the set of entities identified by the head alone. Such phrases are exemplified in (1a) below. But there are at least two further kinds of attribution which are not intersective: these are intensional and subsective (Siegel 1980; Bouchard 2002), exemplified in (1b) and (1c) respectively:

(1)   (a)   beautiful picture
              well-prepared students
              carnivorous animal

       (b)   self-styled genius
              false friend
              future president

       (c)   beautiful dancer
              heavy smoker
              old friend

Intensional attribution (1b) is not intersective in that, for example, *self-styled genius* does not denote the intersection of a set of self-styled people and a set of geniuses: a self-styled genius is not actually a genius. Similarly it is a defining characteristic of a false friend that such a person is not actually a friend. Rather, it seems to be a feature of the lexical semantics of such adjectives that in some form or another they augment the lexical semantics of the head with the feature 'not actual'.

Intensional attribution will not be of further relevance to this study;

but subsective attribution will. The examples in (1c) are ambiguous. They allow not only intersective readings (for example 'dancer who is a beautiful person') but also subsective readings whereby a beautiful dancer may be someone who dances beautifully without necessarily being beautiful. *Beautiful* may modify *dancer* or, apparently, the verb *dance* embedded in *dancer*. Similarly, a heavy smoker may not be a heavy person but just someone who smokes heavily. *Heavy smoker* does not then represent the intersection of the set of heavy objects (or people) and the set of smokers.

While in the attributive position a subsective reading may well be favoured over an intersective one, corresponding predicate constructions (*this dancer is beautiful, this smoker is heavy* etc.) tend to be unambiguous in that they correspond to the intersective reading of the attribute. Indeed there seems generally to be a tendency for the predicate construction to be available only to adjectives with intersective interpretations, or to enforce such interpretations. Probably this is due to the copula *be* and the nature of the semantic relationship it establishes between subject and predicate. Note that the examples of intensional attribution given in (1b) have no predicate equivalents either: **this genius is self-styled.* Predicate constructions must have intersective interpretations.

Subsective attribution has received much attention in research subsequent to Siegel's (1980) influential dissertation (see e.g. Pustejovsky 1995; Jackendoff 1997; Bouchard 2002). The details of the analysis are not as relevant here as is the consensus regarding the general approach: namely that subsectiveness is not encoded in the lexical semantics of the adjective. If the attribute were responsible for the ambiguity then multiple adjectival polysemy would have to be posited to accommodate the ambiguity of *beautiful dancer*, or to express the particular senses of *good* in *good book, good road, good writer* etc. But this polysemy would merely duplicate information already contained in the head's lexical semantics.

The site of the semantic complexity giving rise to such ambiguity is the head rather than the attribute. Pustejovsky (1995) argues that the semantics of the head noun includes sub-elements ('qualia'), such that in *good book* and *good road*, the attribute modifies specifically the qualia 'for reading' and 'for travelling on', contained in the respective heads *book* and *road*. Similarly, Katz and Postal (1964) had previously proposed that the semantics of evaluative adjectives, which often figure in subsective attribution, relates only to an evaluative marker present in the semantics of the head. So, while intersective attribution affects the entire lexical semantics of the head, subsective attribution intersects merely with part of the semantics of the head. In an intersective reading, *beautiful* modifies *dancer* at the highest possible level of generality, which is 'person'. Subsectively, *beautiful* merely modifies the 'dance' feature of *dancer*.

It is therefore also not the case that *beautiful* modifies some morphosyntactic entity (in the present example, the verb *dance*) embedded in the noun. If that were so then an ambiguity of the kind shown in *beautiful dancer* would be wrongly predicted not to occur for example in *beautiful chef*, where there is no embedded verb but the lexeme nevertheless has an activity-denoting element in its lexical semantics. It is that element which is referred to under subsective modification. This detail is important under a lexicalist analysis. As I noted above, lexicalism posits a sharp divide between the syntax and the morphology, such that syntactic operations can affect words but not a specific element of a word's morphological structure, because that structure is invisible to the syntax. Therefore, the difference between intersective and subsective modification cannot under lexicalism be a morphosyntactic matter; the theory correctly predicts it to be a semantic matter.

The dichotomy of intersective vs. subsective attribution is linked to another property of attribution, namely ascriptiveness. Ascriptive attributes ascribe a property to their heads, as (again) in *beautiful picture*. This will be discussed in section 1.2.3 below; suffice it to say at this point that ascriptive attribution occurs among certain noun-plus-noun forms, which may (or may not) be compounds and therefore of lexical origin, such as *fighter-bomber*, *carrier bag*, *stone wall*; and with it comes, in these cases, intersectiveness.

Subsective dependency, though not subsective modification, has a lexical counterpart in the so-called synthetic compounds (*watch-maker*, *coach-driver*, *basket-weaver*). In this class of compounds the first noun, complement rather than modifier to the second, is an argument to a predicate contained in the second, essentially an object to a transitive verb morphosyntactically or semantically contained in the second noun. (I take no view on this here, but see Lieber 1983; van Santen 1986.) Subsectiveness is another feature, then, which straddles the lexicon–syntax divide. We will shortly see more.

1.2.2 *Restrictive vs. non-restrictive attribution*

Adjectival attribution, both intersective and subsective, is subject to a further, recurrent type of ambiguity. Consider the two interpretations typically available to phrases such as those in (1a) above: *the well-prepared students*: 'those students who are well prepared (but not the others)', as opposed to 'the students, who incidentally are all well prepared'. Similarly, *beautiful picture* can mean 'the particular picture which is beautiful' or 'the picture, which incidentally is beautiful'. The source of such well-known ambiguities lies in the distinction between restrictive and non-restrictive modification, often discussed in connection with relative clauses (exemplified by the paraphrases given above) but also present in adjectival attributes (Jespersen 1924: ch. 8; Quirk et al. 1985: ch. 17; Ferris 1993: ch. 7; Pullum and Huddleston 2002).

Like the distinction between intersective and subsective attribution, but unlike further distinctions present among possible attribute–head relationships which will be discussed below, the restrictive–non-restrictive distinction is not a matter of the lexical semantics of the adjective itself. Rather it is, with the exception of one special case, driven by presupposition and perhaps other aspects of pragmatics. The special case is this. An unambiguously non-restrictive interpretation of an attribute arises automatically in the perhaps unusual case where the meaning of the attribute also forms an integral part of the lexical semantics of the head, as for example in *carnivorous lions*. There are no herbivorous lions: the set of lions is a proper subset of the set of carnivorous animals. Carnivorousness is therefore part of the definition of *lion*. This is then a special case of intersectiveness, namely one where the whole of the set denoted by the head constitutes the intersection of the two sets. As *carnivorous lions* denotes the intersection of the set of lions and the set of carnivorous animals, non-restrictive attribution is, like restrictive attribution, a sub-category of intersective attribution. *[handwritten: ? Contradictory]*

On the other hand, where the head's lexical semantics is unspecified for the meaning of the adjective, ambiguity with regard to (non-)restrictiveness will arise, largely driven by pragmatics and presupposition. Thus, a sentence such as *the well-prepared students will pass this exam* is ambiguous. The set of students, already limited by presupposition to those sitting a particular exam (and hence not comprising the whole, generic set of people who are students), may or may not be assumed in its entirety to be well prepared. If this is indeed assumed then the interpretation of *the well-prepared students* is again non-restrictive; if it is not – if therefore the set is assumed also to contain ill-prepared members – then a restrictive interpretation will arise.

It would appear that attribution occurring in the lexicon – in compounds, that is – is invariably restrictive, such that every endocentric compound noun is a hyponym of its head noun. Thus, *coach-driver* denotes a particular kind of driver, *engine oil* a particular kind of oil and left-headed *governor general* a particular kind of governor.

One conclusion to be drawn here, provisionally, is that the semantics of attribution even among constructions originating in the syntax is not necessarily fully compositional (Bouchard 2002: 6 ff.). Full compositionality is present in intersective attribution with restrictive interpretation (*beautiful picture*), as well as perhaps in the special case of invariably context-free non-restrictive intersection (*carnivorous lion*). But importantly, both the specific lexical semantics of the attribute (as in intensional attribution: *self-styled genius*) and the scope of the attribute over the lexical semantics of the head (*beautiful dancer*) may give rise to non-intersective, and hence less-than-fully compositional, semantics. Moreover, pragmatics is involved where lexical semantics is not, in the crucial interpretive difference between restrictive and non-restrictive interpretations in *the well-prepared students.*

The distinction to be discussed next, before turning to matters lexical, is possibly the most important (for present purposes) within the function of attribution. This is the difference in the semantics and syntax of *beautiful picture* and *mental picture, severe decay* and *dental decay.* To understand this difference is to understand the nature of compounding.

1.2.3 *Ascriptive vs. associative attribution*

Typical adjectives are ascriptive. They denote properties, ascribing those properties in intersective attribution to the entity instantiated by the head noun (Ferris 1993: 24) or, in the case of subsective attribution, to a specific semantic feature of that noun. In *beautiful picture, beautiful dancer*, the adjective ascribes the property of being beautiful to a picture or a dancer, or to the way that dancer dances. Together with intersectiveness, ascription constitutes the unmarked, default form of adjectival attribution. I will argue below that adjectival attribution is itself the unmarked form of attribution at least in the syntax (if not in the lexicon), but that ascriptive attribution can also be expressed by nouns, as in *boy actor, silk shirt, olive oil.*

A number of instances have materialised so far where adjectives fail to conform to one or more aspects of prototypical behaviour. Thus, *dead* and *alive* are not gradable; nor will they readily permit modification. The latter moreover cannot occur in the attributive position (**an alive animal*). *Self-styled* is not intersective: a self-styled genius is not a genius. Such failure of certain members of a linguistic category to conform absolutely to prototypical behaviour is hardly surprising. But if an identifiable and substantial subset of the members of the category absolutely fails to conform to the category's defining characteristics, then we have either cause for alarm or an opportunity to learn something fundamental about the grammar of that linguistic category.

One such case is that of the associative adjectives in English, exemplified in (2):

(2)   dental decay
        mental picture
        bovine tuberculosis
        electrical engineer
        rural policeman
        papal murder
        vernal equinox

Such adjectives are neither ascriptive nor intersective. They do not express properties ascribed to, and intersecting with, the denotation of the head noun: there is no property of 'dentalness' that might be ascribed to *decay*. Instead, and non-prototypically where the semantics of adjectives is concerned, associative adjectives denote entities, not properties. In the attribute–head configuration of *dental decay*, the entity denoted by *dental* (namely teeth) is aligned with the denotation of the head noun, so that the meaning 'decay associated with teeth' follows from the attribute–head relationship. Thus, *dental* does not describe the nature of the decay (as ascriptive adjectives such as *slow* or *unexpected* would) but identifies what is decaying: teeth. The properties of associative attribution are discussed in detail for example in Pullum and Huddleston (2002: 556 ff.), Ferris (1993: ch. 2) and Giegerich (2005a).

Unlike those authors (and with more conviction than I did in Giegerich 2005a), I take the view here that the feature 'associated with', which recurs in all associative attribution, is a feature of the attribute–head relationship. There are two types of attribution, ascriptive and associative, and these are at least potentially in parallel, non-redundant distribution. If that were not the case then there could be no contrast between for example *toy fáctory*, which has ascriptive attribution ('factory which is a toy'), and *tóy factory*, where attribution is associative ('factory associated with toys'). This fact will play an important role in later chapters. So, if it is the case that adjectives prototypically denote properties, as *beautiful* does, and that non-prototypically they denote entities, as *dental* does, then we have an explanation for the fact that adjectives can occur in both ascriptive and associative attribution: their lexical semantics predicts the kind of attribution in which they are able to occur. This is what I shall mean by 'ascriptive adjective' and 'associative adjective' in the following chapters. Moreover, the example of the *toy factory* doublet shows that the same can be said for nouns, although the prototypical behaviour for nouns is the denotation of entities. I return to this matter presently.

Associative attribution cannot be non-restrictive (Ferris 1993: 121). A non-restrictive attribute expresses separately one of several properties present in the lexical semantics of the head noun – in *carnivorous lion*, the adjective singles out one of the features which serve to define *lion*. Associative attribution, on the other hand, does not express properties. In the relationship that characterises associative attribution, namely 'associated with X' (for example with teeth, in the case of *dental*), non-restrictiveness would automatically give rise to tautology if the head noun already implied that association: hence **dental dentist*, **dental tooth-ache*.

In addition to their inability to be non-restrictive, associative adjectives violate not only the prototypical characteristics of adjectives – namely ascriptiveness and intersectiveness – but, as I shall show in the next chapter, all the other criteria of prototypical adjectival behaviour as well. Indeed, I shall argue in some detail that associative adjectives represent

a category mismatch, such that they are adjectives with nominal semantics, and that their non-standard behaviour follows largely from this
fact. Associative attribution is prototypically expressed by nouns – note
for example the synonymy of *dental* and *tooth* in *tooth decay*. More
powerful arguments for this position will be presented below.

A converse but essentially similar category mismatch is present in cases
where nouns function as ascriptive attributes (*boy actor*, *silk shirt*, *olive
oil*). The two mismatches form a single picture: in both cases, the attributes tend to display syntactic behaviour inconsistent with that expected of
their respective lexical category. I hope to show that this deficient syntactic
behaviour is explained by invoking the lexicon–syntax split. Ascriptive
attribution is essentially a syntactic phenomenon, prototypically expressed
by adjectives, but may be lexical and may be expressed by nouns.
Associative attribution is essentially a lexical phenomenon, prototypically
expressed by nouns, but may be syntactic and may be expressed by adjectives. Associative attribution is, as I show in the following chapters, the key
to our understanding of compounds and their behaviour.

1.3 The stress patterns of attribution

It has often been claimed or assumed that all phrases – in particular the
attribute-plus-noun constructions that keep figuring in discussions as to
what is or what is not a compound noun – invariably have end-stress. In
addition, there is a slightly less strong research tradition which asserts
that all compounds have fore-stress (for example Bloomfield 1933;
Chomsky and Halle 1968; Marchand 1969; Liberman and Prince 1977;
Liberman and Sproat 1992). If both these claims were correct then the
discussion as to what constitutes a compound and what a phrase would
never have arisen.

Others (for example Halle and Keyser 1971; Olsen 2000; Giegerich
1992, 2004, 2009b; Plag 2006) have argued that, like phrases, compounds may have end-stress. I deal with this issue in Chapters 3 and 5
below, noting here merely that in that case, phrasal end-stress is arguably
the postlexical equivalent of end-stress among compounds – another
phenomenon which straddles the lexicon–syntax divide.

The claim of invariable end-stress for phrases has received rather less
discussion in the phonological literature than that of invariable fore-
stress for compounds. It is expressed for example in the Nuclear Stress
Rule of generative and subsequently metrical phonology (Chomsky and
Halle 1968; Halle and Keyser 1971; Liberman and Prince 1977) and the
American structuralist tradition preceding it, consistent with the more
general assumption that there is such a thing as 'normal stress'.

I shall show in Chapter 3 that this claim is just as wrong as that of
invariable fore-stress for compounds. It is possible for phrasal units

to have fore-stress, and that not just under conditions of 'contrast' or 'emphasis' (Bolinger 1972) – conditions under which stress can be placed deliberately on any syllable as in *I said déported, not éxported*.

Here are some examples of phrasal fore-stress, to be discussed in detail in Chapter 3:

(3) (a) This is the dóctor I was telling you about.
     (b) This is the doctor I was télling you about.
     (c) The well-prepáred students will pass the exam.
     (d) *The carnívorous lions don't eat grass.

Examples (3a.b), from Schmerling (1976: 55), simply belong in different pragmatic contexts. Note that neither version is in any way more 'normal' than the other. Stress on *well-prepared* in (3c) resolves the sentence's ambiguity regarding (non-)restrictiveness in favour of a restrictive interpretation: with this stress pattern the attribute cannot be non-restrictive. And that is why in (3d), the same stress pattern is ill-formed: it enforces a restrictive in a noun phrase whose modifier cannot have that interpretation (Giegerich 2012).

1.4 Summary: the nature of adjectival attribution

The purpose of this chapter has been to identify the principal characteristics of the attribute–head relationship which characterises not only noun phrases containing pre-modifiers but also – as will be discussed in much more detail below – the relationship between the elements of most AdjN and NN compounds.

Attributes denote properties or entities. It follows from the lexical semantics typically associated with adjectives and nouns that, again typically, the former kind of attribution is performed by adjectives, and the latter by nouns. This chapter has been primarily concerned with adjectival attribution; nominal attribution has so far only been mentioned in passing. Property attribution is 'ascriptive' while entity attribution is 'associative', as in *beautiful picture* and *dental decay* respectively. These two basic relationships between the head and the attribute follow to some extent from the property–entity distinction in the lexical semantics of the attribute. But in principle they are subject to independent specification in the attribute–head relationship; and the same pair of lexemes can be concatenated so as to give rise to either ascription or association – recall the two stress variants of *toy factory*.

Ascriptive attribution is typically intersective, such that the entity denoted by the construction represents the intersection of the entities denoted by the head with those that have the property denoted by the adjective. *Beautiful picture* denotes the intersection of the set of pictures and the set of beautiful objects. Non-intersective attribution may be subsective (*heavy smoker, old friend*) or intensional (*self-styled genius*), the latter not relevant below in this study. A subsective attribute ascribes a property merely to a certain aspect of the semantics of the head – for example to the way a smoker smokes. Such constructions are often ambiguous with regard to intersective or subsective interpretation. (A heavy smoker may be a heavy person; an old friend may be a friend of long standing or a friend who is old.) Among lexical constructions, subsective dependency is found in synthetic compounds such as *watch-maker, coach-driver*.

Finally, attribution may be restrictive or non-restrictive. In *carnivorous lion*, the attribute is non-restrictive in that the property it denotes is part of the lexical semantics of the head – all lions are carnivorous. In other cases – *well-prepared students* etc. – the restrictive–non-restrictive distinction is drawn by means of presupposition and other aspects of pragmatics: in isolation, the phrase is ambiguous in that the students in question may or may not be independently known to be well prepared. If they are, then the attribute is non-restrictive. Comparable lexical constructions typically have restrictive attribution: compounds are hyponyms of their heads.

Restrictiveness in attribution also has a bearing on the stress patterns of noun phrases: phrasal fore-stress is possible in restrictive attribution but ill-formed for all non-restrictive attributes. This theme will resurface in Chapter 3; for the moment I merely note that the link between restrictiveness and fore-stress provides us with an intriguing instance of lexicon–syntax continuity.

The full range of distinctions summarised in the preceding paragraphs is available only to the most typical forms of attributes, namely ascriptive adjectival attributes. Associative attribution cannot be non-restrictive; nor can it be intersective. Its failure to be intersective is moreover connected with, and arguably responsible for, the fact that associative (entity-denoting) adjectives cannot be predicates: **This decay is dental.* This deficiency and others connected with associative attribution will be discussed in more detail in the following chapter. There I will make the first attempt at identifying the syntax–lexicon divide within the grammar of attribute–head constructions, which range, as we have seen, from the most productive patterns of intersective adjectival ascription to the deficient associative pattern. While it will become clear that associative attribution is typically lexical (while ascriptive attribution is typically a matter of the syntax), and indeed a central feature of most nominal compounding, we will also observe the occurrence of most of the other features of attribution, as they have been identified in this chapter, on either side of the lexicon–syntax divide.

Chapter 2

Associative attribution

2.1 Introduction: more on ascription and association

We saw in the preceding chapter that one of the functional distinctions that can be drawn among attributes is that between ascriptive and associative attributes. Given that 'attribute' is itself a functional notion, performed by nouns and adjectives (and possibly their phrasal equivalents), the terms 'ascriptive' and 'associative', too, refer to syntactic functions. It is then a separate question what exactly the (sub-)categorial nature of those adjectives and nouns is that serve in ascriptive and associative attribution respectively: sub-category labels such as 'associative adjective' and the like do not imply that associativeness among adjectives, for example, is a categorial label. Rather, such terms are short, for example, for 'adjectives which for semantic reasons can function as associative attributes (only)'. That particular sub-category of adjectives is of considerable interest especially in the context of the present discussion; and I return to it in the following sections. But before going into this kind of detail I will outline more generally, following on from section 1.2.3 above, the ascriptive/associative distinction within attribution.

In ascriptive attribution, the attribute denotes a property which it ascribes to the head noun (Ferris 1993: 24). Property-denoting lexemes are typically, though not exclusively, members of the category Adjective; and indeed such property-denoting adjectives *ceteris paribus* display the prototypical behaviour of adjectives in that, for example, they occur in both attribute and predicate positions (*a nice person – the person is nice*), and they are usually subject to suppletive, morphological or syntactic gradation (*better, nicer, more punctual*).

But the function of being ascriptive attributes to head nouns can also be performed by nouns. Such noun-plus-noun ('NN') combinations, which are often end-stressed, constitute the bulk of what Marchand (1969: 24 ff.) calls 'syntactic groups' (as opposed to compound nouns, which in his, far from uncontroversial, analysis are invariably characterised by forestress). I shall show in Chapter 3 that stress is not at all a reliable diagnostic in the distinction between compounds and phrases: while it is the case that NNs containing ascriptive attributes clearly favour end-stress, and conversely that associative attribution even more clearly favours fore-stress (examples to be given below), there are counterexamples going both ways, which marginalise stress as a diagnostic for compound status overall. They do not, however, disconnect stress entirely from the distinction between ascriptive and associative attribution, as we will see.

A more reliable diagnostic for ascriptiveness among nouns is their ability to be paraphrased as predicates – an ability which follows from the nature of ascription. Consider the examples of ascriptive attribution given in (1):

(1)   baby girl
       toy train
       boy actor
       luxury flat
       bottom line

Such NNs are subject to paraphrase as 'a girl who is a baby', 'a train which is a toy' etc., such that being a baby is a property ascribed to the girl, being a toy is a property ascribed to the train etc.

Similarly, ascriptive attribution is present in NNs where the attribute denotes material, as in (2):

(2)   steel bridge
       stone wall
       silk shirt
       gold watch
       leather glove

For such NNs, paraphrase as a predicate ('this bridge is steel') is perhaps not as readily available to all speakers as it is in the cases listed in (1); but this uncertainty concerns the lexical category of *steel* rather than the nature of the attribution: it is not entirely obvious that the attributes in these examples are nouns.

In the derivational morphology, *-en* attaches to nouns denoting material and produces adjectives denoting 'made of . . .', as in *wooden, woollen*. However, it seems that these two examples are now the only ones available: adjective-forming *-en* is no longer productive in English (Marchand 1969: 270 f.). Formations such as **bricken, steelen, stonen* are ill-formed; and forms such as *golden, silken, leaden* are now possible under metaphorical interpretations only (*golden wedding, silken voice*). Non-metaphorical senses denoting 'made of' are expressed by *gold watch, silk shirt, lead pipe*, where the attribute may be treated as a noun, or as an adjective converted from a noun (as a productive default to the listed outcomes of adjective-forming *-en*), or perhaps as an instance of a context-specifically suspended category contrast. Nothing depends on this issue here; what is clear is that attributes such as those in (2) are ascriptive just as those expressed straightforwardly by adjectives in *wooden bridge, woollen sweater* are.

A similar case is presented by place-names such as *Edinburgh, London* etc. occurring in *Edinburgh student, London taxi*. Pairs denoting 'place' vs. 'provenance' are available in English for countries (*England – English, Belgium – Belgian, Japan – Japanese*) but not regularly for towns. (Irregular forms such as *Glaswegian, Aberdonian, Londoner* etc. tend to denote persons specifically.) In such cases, *Edinburgh* is probably an adjective for those speakers for whom *this student is Edinburgh* is grammatical, but neither the grammaticality of the paraphrase nor the question of whether the attribute is really a noun affects the fact that these are further examples of ascriptive attribution, this time denoting 'provenance'. Forms such as *English, Belgian* etc. display the same categorial ambiguity, of course: compare *a Belgian car* (where *Belgian* is an adjective) with *the Belgians are* ... (where the inflectional morphology identifies *Belgian* as a noun); and compare further *the English are* ... vs. **the Englishes are* ... (in the sense of 'people from England'). Again, this is not an issue which needs resolving here. What counts is the invariably ascriptive nature of any attributive function that such lexemes engage in.

There is, however, another possible ambiguity among attributes, more relevant in the present context than that involving lexical category status. This is the ambiguity involving ascriptive vs. associative attribution: as we will see below, certain adjectives and certain nouns can function as either.

Ascriptive attribution, then, is typically performed by adjectives but also available to certain nouns. In contrast, associative attribution is typically performed by nouns but also available to certain adjectives. The reason for the preponderance of nouns in associative attribution is that such attributes denote entities, rather than properties, with which the head is in some way associated; and entities are typically denoted by nouns (Ferris 1993: 19 ff.; Pullum and Huddleston 2002: 525 ff.). Some examples are given in (3):

(3)   tooth brush
       cattle disease
       school bus
       milk-tooth
       hair net

A tooth brush is a brush associated with teeth, a cattle disease is a disease associated with cattle; and so on. A milk-tooth is a tooth in some way associated with milk, although the precise nature of this association may well be unclear. Such NNs constitute the mainstream of nominal compounding; and it is possible for compounds (as it is for any other kind of lexical item) to be semantically non-transparent.

⌊Clearly, the 'associated with' relationship holding between head and attribute in such cases is semantically very versatile, amenable to a wide range of specific interpretations which relate to the speaker's encyclopedic knowledge.⌋ A tooth brush is associated with teeth in that it is designed to clean them; a cattle disease is a disease associated with cattle in that it affects them; a school bus is a bus associated with schools in that it carries pupils to and from them; and so on. Ascriptive attribution does not have this degree of semantic versatility; certainly it is not amenable to non-transparency in the way associative attribution is.

Consider now the examples given in (4): all these are stress doublets (first discussed by Faiß 1981) which have fore-stress or end-stress depending on their semantic interpretations:

(4)   toy factory
       steel warehouse
       hair net
       glass case
       driving instructor

In each of these examples, the fore-stressed version is characterised by associative attribution while end-stress goes with ascription. Thus, *tóy factory* means 'factory associated with (specifically: producing) toys' while *toy fáctory* means 'factory which is a toy'. With fore-stress, *steel warehouse* means 'warehouse associated with, and specifically storing, steel' while the end-stressed version denotes a warehouse made of steel – recall further examples of this nature given in (2) above. Similarly a hair net can be, depending on its stress, a net for the control of hair (associative) or a net made of hair (ascriptive). *Tooth brush*, with end-stress indicating ascription, would denote a brush made out of a tooth. And with fore-stress a driving instructor is an instructor associated with driving, while under end-stress it denotes an instructor who is driving. Stress doublets such as that do not constitute some closed set of dual lexicalisations differentiated by stress: this is an open set connected with productive processes.

In the same vein compare *Edinburgh student*, discussed earlier, and *Edinburgh train*. The former is likely to have an ascriptive interpretation, as we saw, although an associative interpretation is also possible – a student associated with Edinburgh in that she or he studies Edinburgh. *Edinburgh train*, on the other hand, is likely to have an associative interpretation in that it is a train either to or from Edinburgh. Ascriptive

Edinburgh student has end-stress; but for associative *Edinburgh train*, fore-stress is at least available.

I discuss stress and its relation to the ascriptive–associative distinction in more detail later in this chapter and especially in the next chapter. But it is already clear, not least from examples such as those in (4) above, that the distinction between ascriptive and associative attribution is key to our understanding of (at least nominal) compounding; and specifically it is key to our understanding of compound stress. Given the clarity and recurrence with which the stress contrast signals the contrast in the nature of attribution, there must be a causal connection, however complicated, between these two apparently unrelated phenomena.

It has been said that the difference between ascriptive and associative attribution is hard to draw in certain cases: Bauer et al. (2013: 447) cite the example of *door knob*. But *door* in this example is not a property ascribed to *knob* but an entity with which the knob is associated. This is also shown by the impossibility of **this knob is door*, a reliable diagnostic of ascriptive attribution, as I noted in section 1.2.3 above.

I turn now to associative attribution performed not by nouns, as in (3) above, but by adjectives as in (5):

(5)   dental decay
        bovine disease
        vernal equinox
        criminal law
        solar panel

Associative adjectives such as these, synonymous with nouns as in *tooth decay, cattle disease, spring equinox* etc., are the subject of the following sections. This discussion will also raise questions regarding the locus of the two kinds of attribution in the grammar – when exactly is attribution, ascriptive or associative, 'lexical', giving rise to compound nouns, and when is it syntactic, creating phrasal units? But before addressing the role played in the grammar of attribution by an assumed modular division between the syntax and the lexicon, and the problems associated with such a division, I want to discuss here the behaviour of 'associative adjectives' in some more detail.

2.2 The morphology and lexical semantics of associative adjectives

Recall that these are adjectives which denote entities, and which in attributive usage establish the relationship of 'associated with' between the head and the attribute. *Dental decay* is 'decay associated with teeth', synonymous with *tooth decay*. The adjective *dental* is therefore synonymous with the noun *tooth*. Similarly, *bodily harm* is harm associated with the body. While in that instance the synonym *body harm* is well-formed but unlikely to be used, we may expect the existence of a synonymous noun to be a reliable diagnostic of an associative adjective. Recall also that associative attributes cannot turn into predicates, unlike ascriptive attributes.

Drawing on work by Levi (1978), Leitzke (1989), Ferris (1993) and others, the following discussion will be concerned in turn with the morphological, semantic and syntactic properties of associative adjectives that are relevant here. The distinction between associative and ascriptive senses, between entity-denoting and property-denoting adjectives, is both subtle and important. It is, as we shall see, subtle not least because of widespread ambiguity involving associative and ascriptive senses. And it is important not only because it will figure crucially in the further discussion below of the syntactic behaviour of such adjectives, but also because it will be central to our understanding of compounds.

If we assume, then, that adjectives prototypically denote properties – these are the ascriptive, 'mainstream' adjectives discussed earlier – and that nouns prototypically denote entities, then the entity-denoting, associative adjectives under discussion here constitute a mismatch between a lexical category and the semantics typically associated with it. This gives rise to non-prototypical behaviour.

Another example of a category mismatch involving entity vs. property denotation, relevant here in more ways than one, is that of the abstract nouns in English (*chastity*, *warmth*, *coolness*, *pride*). Abstract nouns are in some way the mirror image of associative adjectives: while the latter are entity-denoting adjectives, the former are property-denoting nouns. Such non-prototypical semantics has syntactic consequences: unlike count nouns, which denote entities, abstract nouns can neither pluralise nor take indefinite determiners (**two chastities*, **a health*). We shall see similar, non-prototypical syntactic behaviour on the part of associative adjectives below.

Many of the abstract nouns are formed with the rival suffixes *-ity*, *-th* and *-ness*, as in some of the examples given above; and it is not surprising that all such suffixes are deadjectival: they derive from property-denoting bases. Conversely, derived associative adjectives are always denominal. But alongside such morphologically complex cases there are also synchronically underived abstract nouns such as *pride* and *greed*. Moreover, many *-ity* and *-th* nouns appear to have drifted semantically into the more mainstream count noun class – *an opportunity*, *two fatalities*, *three lengths of the pool* – so that it may be argued that property denotation among nouns is not only non-prototypical but also perhaps unstable. Such behaviour is mirrored by associative adjectives, as we shall see.

If this comparison holds then there is no reason to expect a single derivational suffix to be responsible for the formation of all associative adjectives in English; nor should such adjectives be expected always to be morphologically derived at all. The widespread existence in the language of rival processes, often involving competition between Latinate and non-Latinate suffixes, is well known (Plag 1999; Giegerich 2001). The range of associative adjectives within the morphology of English is similar, but the number of derivational suffixes said to be involved, regularly or occasionally, in the production of such adjectives is striking. Leitzke (1989: 16) claims that there are nineteen such suffixes, of which five are of Germanic origin. I cite Leitzke's list in (6) below, to illustrate her point rather than to endorse it wholesale.

(6) (a) Latinate | | (b) Germanic
-al/-ar	criminal, polar		-en	wooden
-an	urban		-ern	southern
-ary	visionary		-ish	childish
-ate	collegiate		-ly	bodily
-ese	Japanese		-y	fatty
-esque	Dantesque			
-fic	Pacific			
-ic/-ac	atomic, cardiac			
-ine	feminine			
-ist	socialist			
-ite	Israelite			
-ive	secretive			
-ory	illusory			
-ous	nervous			

Leitzke's list is in part unconvincing in that many of her examples have alternative, and often more predominant, ascriptive senses (*criminal, visionary, socialist, . . .*); indeed in cases such as *wooden*, all reasonable interpretations, literal or metaphorical, are ascriptive, as we saw above. Moreover, it is unclear whether all the adjectival endings listed in (6a) are really derivational suffixes in the synchronic morphology. I return to this issue below. What is compelling, however, is the generalisation whereby any category-changing derivation found in (6) is always denominal. Given the entity-denoting nature of associative adjectives, this is as unsurprising as is the deadjectival nature of derivations yielding abstract nouns, noted earlier.

In addition, just as in the case of the abstract nouns mentioned earlier, there is a substantial class of (in this case Latinate) adjectives which do not derive synchronically from nouns (or from any other identifiable base) but which 'partner' nouns in semantic terms. These 'collateral adjectives' (Koshiishi 2002, 2011) are exemplified in (7) with their nominal partners:

(7)   equine – horse
       feline – cat
       phocine – seal
       bovine – cattle
       dental – tooth
       mental – mind
       vernal – spring

The distinction between 'derived' and 'underived' adjectives is in many cases an artefact of the theory of derivational morphology deployed for its expression; certainly it is, as it should be under lexicalist assumptions, irrelevant to other aspects of the behaviour of such adjectives. *Urban* and *feminine* in Leitzke's list – (6a) above – belong under (7) if the group of collateral adjectives is recognised separately, as it is by Koshiishi (2002). Unlike Leitzke's *Pacific*, they do contain recurrent adjectival endings but their bases are not necessarily recurrent. These adjectives cannot therefore realistically be regarded as synchronically derived, if derivation is assumed, fairly uncontroversially, to operate strictly on the form side. Koshiishi treats the relationships such as that between *urban* and *town*, *feline* and *cat*, which characterises the class of collaterals, as suppletion, implying therefore a predominantly semantically based synchronic derivational relationship akin to that generally accepted in the inflectional morphology (where 'suppletion' figures routinely).

Moreover, the suffixes on display in (6a) above are probably without exception unproductive in English, so that all such adjectives are part of the 'listed morphology' of the language which in a stratified lexicon characterises the first stratum (see Giegerich 1999: ch. 3). The same case can be made separately regarding the semantics of such adjectives, as we shall see, as well as regarding the associative senses occurring with the Germanic suffixes in (6b). It is striking that there is no single morphological process in present-day English which productively generates associative adjectives and only those. Nor is there a less-than-fully productive adjective-forming suffix whose outputs are invariably associative. Rather, entity-denoting senses are found among adjectives in many productive, unproductive, fossilised, native and non-native outcomes of the denominal morphology of English, often alongside property-denoting senses.

A possible reason for this haphazard occurrence of associative senses in the derivational morphology of adjectives is that associative adjectives tend to be unstable in English (Leitzke 1989: ch. 4; Giegerich 2005a; Shore 2010). Many of the adjectives involved in (6) and (7) may display ascriptive (and with those, intersective) senses alongside their associative senses, often predominantly so. There is no difference in behaviour between the two groups (6) and (7) in this respect, or indeed in any other respect.

Of the suffixes in (6), -al forms an ascriptive adjective in *criminal gang* while the same adjective is associative in *criminal law*, and ambiguous (albeit perhaps facetiously so) in *criminal lawyer*. Similarly, *musical* is ascriptive in *musical child* and associative in *musical director* – observe again how associative interpretations allow paraphrase by nouns while ascriptive interpretations do not allow this: *music theory* vs. **music child*. In *John's Japanese adventure*, *Japanese* is associative ('adventure associated with Japan', 'Japan adventure') while in *Japanese car*, *Japanese child*, the adjective has the ascriptive sense 'originating from Japan' and cannot be paraphrased by a noun (**Japan car*). *Fatty* is associative in *fatty acid* ('acid associated with fat', 'fat acid') and ascriptive in *fatty soup*. Similarly, *friendly* has an ascriptive sense in most usage (*a friendly person*); but in the collocation *friendly fire*, found in armed forces jargon, the adjective is exceptionally intended to be associative: 'gunfire associated with one's own side'. At least for this one particular collocation – an issue to which I return below – associative *friendly* has to be specifically listed. Associativeness (that is, entity denotation) does not follow automatically from the presence of adjective-forming -ly or any other adjective-forming suffix.

In the same vein, many collateral adjectives have ascriptive senses alongside their primary associative ones. These are often (but not always) metaphorical or figurative: a person may have a feline face; a crowd of people may be bovine in behaviour. But in associative *bovine tuberculosis* ('tuberculosis associated with cattle') there is no connotation of docile or herd-like behaviour. *Dental decay* is decay associated with teeth, but in *dental fricative* the adjective is again ascriptive, denoting a property of a fricative described in terms of its place of articulation.

But even taking into account such possible ambiguity involving ascription and association, as Leitzke does later in her study (1989: 139 ff.), her list of nineteen suffixes able to produce associative adjectives is almost certainly over-inclusive. Some of her examples are in reality ascriptive, as is probably the whole range of adjectives produced by certain suffixes. While she assumes *childish* to mean 'associated with children, relating to children', the meaning is more precisely '*typically* associated with children', so that it is possible for *childish behaviour*, for example, also to be displayed by childish adults. *Childish behaviour* is then not 'behaviour associated with children' but 'behaviour like that associated with children'. *Childish* is ascriptive. Nor do there seem to be any other -ish adjectives that are unequivocally associative.

Similarly, *wooden* means not merely 'associated with wood' but, more precisely, 'made of wood' and is therefore ascriptive. While it is the case that -*en* adjectives now have predominantly metaphorical senses – recall *a silken voice* vs. **a silken shirt, a golden wedding* vs. *a golden watch (Marchand 1969: 270 f.) – such adjectives are no less ascriptive in metaphorical senses than in their material-denoting and hence non-metaphorical instances such as *woollen* are. *Wooden* has both senses, but neither is associative. And similarly again, -*esque* means 'having the style of' (Marchand 1969: 286) rather than simply 'associated with', so that the work of authors other than Dante is more likely to be described as *Dantesque* than is the work of Dante himself. This again makes *Dantesque* an ascriptive adjective.

The examples just discussed demonstrate, then, that it is common for individual associative adjectives also to have (or perhaps to acquire) ascriptive senses, as well as for adjective-forming suffixes to have denotations more specific than simply being associative. Often, as we have seen, such ascription is of a metaphorical nature. In the case of some collateral adjectives such as *bovine* etc., associative senses co-exist with metaphorical ascriptive senses, such that *bovine behaviour* may mean either 'behaviour associated with cattle' or 'behaviour like that associated with cattle' (Leitzke 1989: 139 ff.); in the case of *childish*, an originally associative sense appears to have given way entirely to ascription. *Criminal* has the general, associative sense 'associated with crime' in *criminal law*, as well as denoting a more specific ascriptive sense, namely that of 'committing crime' in *criminal gang*. Similarly, in *dental fricative*, *dental* denotes a specific association with teeth, namely the quality of being produced in their vicinity. These observations are able to be distilled into two conclusions, both of which will be relevant to the argument that follows.

The first conclusion, confirming what we have already seen in an earlier discussion, is that there is no reason to believe associativeness to be encoded as such in the lexical semantics of what I have been calling associative adjectives. Such adjectives simply denote entities rather than properties. In their associative senses, adjectives are synonymous with the nouns from which they synchronically derive (*friend* – *friendly*) or which they partner semantically (*cat* – *feline*). *Feline tuberculosis* and *cat tuberculosis* are synonymous. The relationship of 'associated with' that characterises attribution through associative adjectives is a consequence of the attribute–head configuration. So, an adjective such as *dental* is not inherently associative; it is merely entity-denoting and for that reason capable of associative attribution. As we shall see, attribution is the only function available to associative adjectives.

Suffixes forming associative adjectives are therefore semantically empty (Levi 1978; Kastovsky 1982; Warren 1984). They add nothing to the semantics of the base noun: one might even argue that the noun and 'its' associative adjective are exponents of the same lexical entry (in the sense suggested for the morphology of numerals by Stump 2010).

In contrast, ascription denotes a property. For example, while associative *feline* means 'cat', ascriptive *feline* means 'cat-like'; and more examples of the relationship between associative and ascriptive senses were given above. Ascription implies more specific senses additional to (and often loosely and perhaps metaphorically based on) those of entities, and in the case of derivational suffixes, it therefore implies non-empty semantics. The distinction within attribution between association and ascription reduces to the denotation of entity vs. property among attributes.

Secondly, the very large scale on which ascriptive intersective senses develop in adjectives originally classified (at least by Leitzke 1989) as associative suggests that entity denotation is not the default interpretation even for denominal adjectives in the attribute position. (See here again Shore 2010.) Adjectives with entity-denoting senses in attribution are lexically listed, on formal and/or semantic grounds, and tend to default into ascription. This stands to reason, given the prototypically property-denoting, hence ascriptive, nature of the lexical category Adjective. And this is in turn consistent with the earlier observation whereby associative adjectives are manifestations of a category mismatch. As instances of nominal semantics paired with adjectival morphosyntax, such forms are deficient. I will show below that this deficiency is reflected in, and at least in part explains, the syntactic behaviour of associative adjectives.

2.3 The syntax of associative adjectives

I want to show in this section that, compared to their mainstream ascriptive counterparts, associative adjectives display a number of deficiencies in their syntactic behaviour. Such adjectives cannot be predicates; they cannot be modified; and they are not gradable. They are also prone to individual distributional gaps.

As we saw in Chapter 1, such deficiencies also occur individually with various sub-groups of other adjectives; but here they add up to a coherent set of properties which all seem to relate to the entity-denoting nature of associative adjectives. Moreover, as we shall see, these properties are consistent with a generalisation whereby associative adjectives do not form adjective phrases. This generalisation, viewed together with various restrictions on the part of the heads of AdjNs involving associative adjectives (henceforth 'associative AdjNs') will qualify such constructions for compound-noun – that is, lexical – status. However, as we shall see, to qualify for such status is not necessarily to have such status.

As I discussed in some detail in Chapter 1, prototypical adjectives can be both attributes and predicates, as for example in *beautiful picture – this picture is beautiful*. However, this freedom of distribution is only available where the adjective is ascriptive, and specifically where there is an intersective relationship between the ascriptive adjective and its head: intensional adjectives cannot be predicates (*this genius is self-styled*); nor can a subsective attribute translate into a predicate without thereby adopting an alternative, intersective interpretation, as is shown by both *heavy smoker* and *beautiful dancer* vs. *this smoker is heavy, the dancer is beautiful.*

Given this link between intersectiveness and the predicate position, it is hardly surprising that associative adjectives should equally be unable to function as predicates: associative adjectives constitute a major subclass among the intrinsically non-intersective adjectives. Indeed, when the predicate function is performed by an adjective which is subject to the ascriptive–associative ambiguity discussed above then its interpretation will automatically be ascriptive, as well as intersective. Compare **this decay is dental* and *this fricative is dental* – the latter ascriptive, as also in **this theory is musical* vs. *this child is musical, *this acid is fatty* vs. *this soup is fatty. Criminal lawyer* is ambiguous, but *this lawyer is criminal* is unambiguously ascriptive. Similarly again, where a collateral adjective of the group *bovine, feline, equine* etc. occurs in the predicate position, its sense must be metaphorical and hence ascriptive. Compare *feline tuberculosis* and *feline face*: **this tuberculosis is feline* vs. *his face is feline.* There are two possible explanations for this, one to do with the semantics and the other to do with the syntax of associative adjectives. The two are linked.

On the semantic side, the relationship between entity-denoting *dental* and *decay* is not 'is', as it is in ascriptive *dental fricative*, but 'is associated with'. Hence for *dental decay, musical director, fatty acid, criminal law*, we get *this decay is associated with teeth, this theory is associated with music, this acid . . . with fat, this law . . . with crime.* Such adjectives' failure to occur as predicates is thus directly linked with the entity-denoting nature of associative adjectives.

The same case can be made regarding nominal attributes. A noun which is an ascriptive attribute can translate into a predicate, but this is not possible under associative attribution. Compare ascriptive *tóy fáctory* – *this factory is a toy* and associative *tóy factory* – *this factory is associated with toys.*

As regards the syntactic side of the argument, it is clearly the case that predicates not involving associative adjectives have phrasal status: in *John is very clever, John is a genius*, the predicates are adjective phrases or noun phrases. **John is genius* is ill-formed. It stands to reason, therefore, that in *John is clever*, the predicate is a one-word adjective phrase rather than a mere adjective. If it can be shown that associative adjectives cannot head adjective phrases then this generalisation accounts straightforwardly for their inability to be predicates.

Returning once more to the general properties of adjectives discussed in Chapter 1, recall that members of this category are typically, though not in all instances, amenable to pre-modification by degree adverbs and other adverbs – *very beautiful, surprisingly fast* – and that they have the related feature of either analytic or inflectional gradability (*more beautiful, fastest*). But some specimens of ascriptive adjectives – mostly 'absolute' adjectives such as *complete, correct, dead* etc. (Pullum and Huddleston 2002: 531) – are not gradable and largely resist modification while showing straightforward behaviour in other respects. For example, they freely function as predicates: *this cat is dead.*

Like absolute adjectives, associative adjectives are neither gradable nor in more general terms amenable to modification by degree and other adverbs. One decay cannot be **more dental* than another; *friendlier* and *fattier* are possible only under ascriptive interpretation, as in *a friendlier person, fattier soup*, but not in **friendlier fire,*fattier acid*. Similarly, *distinctly criminal law, a very musical director* impose ascriptive interpretations on the adjective, like those found rather more plausibly in *a distinctly criminal gang* and *a very musical child*.

Deficiencies such as that of being barred from the predicate position, or from modification or gradation, are probably of little significance regarding general category behaviour when they occur in isolation; and we saw in Chapter 1 that small groups of otherwise quite straightforward, ascriptive adjectives may have such small deficiencies in behaviour. Associative adjectives, in contrast, have them all. Indeed, the deficiencies of associative adjectives clearly add up to an inability to form adjective phrases: they cannot occur where phrasal status is required, and they cannot be heads.

However, the alternative semantic explanation given above for the ban on being predicates also holds with regard to the ban on modification. Associative adjectives denote entities; and entities are not gradable and do not come by degrees. The two explanations – denoting of entities and no heading of phrases – are clearly not unrelated; and both in turn relate to the more basic category mismatch displayed by associative adjectives, as adjectives which denote entities rather than properties.

Some support for ranking the semantic explanation above the syntactic one is provided by the fact that the inability to head a phrase accounts for the ungrammaticality of analytical gradation (**more dental*), which builds adjective phrases, but not for the absence of inflectional gradation. Yet, **fattier acid* is equally ruled out. It would appear, therefore, that both the semantic and the syntactic generalisations proposed here are independently valid although they are clearly not unrelated. Both will be relevant later in this study.

While it seems clearly to be the case that associative adjectives cannot be heads of adjective phrases, this characteristic leaves unexplained, at least at face value, some further, important features of their behaviour in addition to their failure to undergo inflectional gradation. Both these aspects have to do with the adjective's behaviour towards its head.

The first such feature is that many associative adjectives attach only to an arbitrarily restricted range of heads, with rival noun-plus-noun constructions being preferred in what seems like the majority of cases. For many speakers, *vernal* occurs only with *equinox* and not for example with *cleaning, cabbage, weather* etc., for which we get *spring cleaning, spring weather* etc. Moreover, the year's other equinox is more likely to be the *autumn equinox*, rather than the *autumnal equinox*. The latter's avoidance may be due to the predominantly ascriptive sense of *autumnal*, for probably most speakers. And some speakers may collocate *vernal* occasionally with nouns other than *equinox*. The *Oxford English Dictionary* gives *shower, bird* and *setting*. Idiolectal variation of this kind is to be expected especially for specialised lexemes such as this one. But regardless of whether this particular adjective collocates for certain speakers with four or even ten different nouns or just with one, the point is that the distribution of *vernal* is severely lexically restricted to specific heads, and that the rival form *spring* collocates freely with any head including those which fail to take *vernal*. While this is not the kind of behaviour we expect of lexemes entering into phrasal constructions, it is behaviour common among associative adjectives.

As another example, *dental* collocates with *care, decay, treatment, floss* etc., but it apparently does not go with *mug* or *brush*, or *fairy*, for which the synonym *tooth* is again preferred. So, associative adjectives are not only interchangeable with nouns in the attribute function (*feline/cat behaviour, phocine/seal distemper, vernal/spring equinox, dental/tooth decay*) – the only function they can perform, as we have seen – but dispreferred to nouns in many other and entirely arbitrary cases.

The second feature of associative adjectives which is not readily explained by their failure to form adjective phrases is that in multiple attribution, associative attributes do not mix freely with ascriptive attributes. It is not only the adjective in associative attribution that is not amenable to syntactic modification (recall *very musical director*): the head in such a structure is subject to a similar, though somewhat more complicated constraint. *Feline contagious tuberculosis, *phocine fatal distemper* are ill-formed, as are *friendly sustained fire, *criminal dead lawyer* under associative interpretations. In linear terms this means that in embedded attribution structures, associative adjectives cannot be followed by ascriptive adjectives, but it does not mean that nothing can intervene between an associative adjective and its head noun. Sequences of associative adjectives, such as *juvenile cardiac arrest, phocine pneumonic disease* etc., are well-formed. This constraint is reminiscent of but, as we shall see, not quite identical to a sequencing restriction which is well known to hold within sequences of ascriptive adjectives: *a wealthy German relative* is preferred to *a German wealthy relative*, *a well-known fatal disease* more likely than *a fatal well-known disease*. The generalisation here is that it is at least unusual for a gradable adjective to be preceded by a non-gradable adjective (Quirk et al. 1985: 437 f.; Payne and Huddleston 2002: 452).

For associative adjectives, which are of course non-gradable, this sequencing preference in the syntax of attribution correctly allows *juvenile cardiac arrest* ('cardiac arrest associated with youth'). But it also allows the reverse order of these adjectives (**cardiac juvenile arrest*); and it fails to account for the ungrammaticality of **phocine fatal distemper* and **criminal dead lawyer*, also sequences of non-gradable adjectives which differ from the former example in that their second adjectives are ascriptive (and as such merely exceptionally non-gradable). So, the known sequencing restriction involving mere gradability does not do all the work required here. Associative adjectives cannot modify heads containing ascriptive attributes. In addition, certain associative adjectives cannot modify heads containing certain other associative adjectives. Note moreover that the general sequencing restriction for adjectives is optional while we are dealing here with an outright ban on certain sequences.

Finally, observe that the sequencing constraint involving ascriptive and associative adjectives also holds where these attribution functions are performed by nouns or by a mixed sequence of nouns and adjectives. Both *Edinburgh linguistics student* and *Scottish linguistics student* are acceptable, while neither **linguistics Edinburgh student* nor **linguistics Scottish student* is. Similar behaviour is found in *steel/wooden railway bridge* vs. **railway steel/wooden bridge*. Moreover, *musical* tends to be associative in *Edinburgh musical director* while it is ascriptive in *musical Edinburgh director*. So, this really seems to be a constraint on sequencing the functions of attribution – associative attribution cannot occur 'outside' ascription – rather than a constraint on lexical category sequences.

We might formulate an ad hoc constraint here to rule out associative attribution with heads containing ascriptive attributes. But given the overlap of such a constraint with the optional sequencing restriction discussed above, such a constraint would be hard to motivate. I shall argue in the next section that such stacking restrictions are better expressed by invoking the lexicon–syntax divide, and that doing so will enable other characteristics of associative adjectives to fall into place.

2.4 Candidature for lexical status

I showed in the preceding section that, compared to ascriptive adjectives, associative adjectives are subject to a number of apparently unrelated constraints on their syntactic behaviour. They can be attributes but not predicates. They are neither gradable nor amenable to modification. They may randomly reject perfectly suitable heads. And where attributes occur in sequence they cannot precede ascriptive attributes.

I tentatively suggested earlier that the first two of these constraints may be accounted for by an analysis whereby associative adjectives, non-prototypical and category-mismatched as they are, do not form adjective phrases. I now want to argue that this failure to become heads of phrases is in turn epiphenomenal to their failure to occur in the syntax: associative AdjNs are lexical; and this accounts for the other two constraints noted above. This is an analysis foreshadowed in essence by Levi (1978).

Such an analysis is strongly suggested by the grammaticality of *vernal equinox*, as opposed to **vernal cabbage*, **vernal cleaning* – AdjNs involving *vernal* are simply lexically listed. But the distributional defectiveness of *vernal* does not prove that all associative adjectives are confined to lexical AdjNs: those not observed to be defectively distributed may be available to the syntax. The sequencing constraint discussed earlier is more revealing in this respect.

Instead of formulating an *ad hoc* constraint to rule out associative attribution with heads containing ascriptive attributes, we might argue that ascriptive adjectives freely attach to their heads under NP while associative adjectives attach under N. Ascriptive AdjNs are then phrases and associative AdjNs are compound nouns in the traditional terminology. This analysis is consistent with our earlier finding whereby associative adjectives are not heads of adjective phrases: we would not expect adjective phrases to occur as attributes under N (or at least so we assume until we revisit this issue in Chapter 5); and certainly we *would* expect attributes under NP to be phrasal.

If that is the case then, moreover, *fatal distemper* and *dead lawyer* (involving non-gradable but ascriptive adjectives) are NPs, unavailable therefore for modification by adjectives with associative senses, such as *phocine* and *criminal*. **Phocine fatal distemper* would constitute an N whose head is an NP. In contrast, *cardiac arrest* and *phocine distemper* are Ns, and therefore amenable to ascriptive attribution at the NP level – *unexpected cardiac arrest*, *fatal phocine distemper* respectively – or to further associative attribution at level N: *juvenile cardiac arrest*. In an account which treats associative AdjNs as $AdjN_N$, this recursiveness arises because *cardiac arrest*, *pneumonic diseases* are themselves associative AdjNs (and hence Ns), which can then be heads within associative AdjNs.

It is not really surprising that associative adjectives should be able to attach, and recursively so, under N. Identical behaviour is shown by noun-plus-noun constructions, whose ability to be synonymous with associative-adjective constructions we have already noted. Thus, *juvenile cardiac disease*, for example, is paralleled by *childhood heart disease*.

As it happens, such NN constructions are widely – and hardly controversially – known to be compounds, for which recursiveness is similarly uncontroversial: compounds can occur inside compounds, but phrases cannot – or so we still assume for the moment. Associative-adjective constructions behave in the same way, though the case for their lexical ('compound') status has yet to be made fully. All we know is that they qualify for that status.

Note, however, that in recursive associative-adjectival as well as nominal concatenation, the dependents are subject to further sequencing restrictions: **heart childhood disease, *cardiac juvenile arrest, *pneumonic phocine disease*. Clearly, there are finer distinctions involved in determining the well-formed stacking of dependents than a lexicon–syntax split whereby all associative attribution – by way of adjectives or nouns – is simply regarded as lexical, and all ascriptive attribution as phrasal. *Cardiac arrest*, for example, is likely to be a listed collocation and for that reason not interruptable by *juvenile*. I return to this issue further below in this book, as part of a more finely grained discussion of 'associativeness' as well as of the purported dividing line between the syntax and the lexicon. For the moment I continue to explore the simple lexicalist analysis of all associative AdjNs, arguing that associative AdjNs at the very least qualify for lexical status. Whether they actually *have* lexical status is then the next question, which I address in the next section.

I want to conclude the present section by arguing that in associative AdjNs, the semantic relationship between the adjective and the head noun is not as predictable – in the sense of transparency, or compositionality – as we would expect it to be if such AdjNs were formed in the syntax. In many cases this relationship is ambiguous, depending crucially on the context as well as encyclopedic knowledge. In (8) below, containing adjectives which denote persons, at least three relationships are exemplified: in (8a) we have the straightforward, (near-)compositional sense of 'associated with', which as we have seen characterises such adjectives. In (8b.c) the adjectives express different arguments – objects and subjects respectively – of a predicate contained in the head noun.

(8)   (a)   papal emissary
              presidential plane
              professorial salary

       (b)   papal murder
              presidential election
              professorial appointment

       (c)   papal visit
              presidential lie
              professorial comment

Note, however, that the object vs. subject interpretations imposed on the phrases in (8b.c) are dependent on speakers' encyclopedic knowledge as well as on established usage, such that the pope is assumed to be less likely to murder anyone than he is to go visiting. Compare *terrorist murder*, where the opposite interpretation seems more likely. And *presidential election* is, like *parliamentary election*, an established term following a recurrent pattern. Nevertheless, the opposite interpretations are feasible in appropriate contexts: *the papal murder of the cardinal, the prime minister's papal visit, the presidential election of the national security advisor, the parliamentary election of the Speaker. Presidential lie* is unambiguous only because *lie* is intransitive.

Such phrases raise interesting structural questions: under a lexical analysis of associative AdjNs, the head of *of the cardinal* must be *papal murder*. But the point is that the interpretations imposed above on (8b.c) are in principle interchangeable; and even in (8a), ambiguity is not really ruled out. Appropriate contextualisation would allow an alternative interpretation for *papal emissary* ('emissary associated with the pope', 'the pope's emissary'), namely 'the emissary who is the pope': *God's papal emissary*.

In (8), the range of possible interpretations seems to be driven by possible syntactic argument structures imposed by deverbal heads (Grimshaw 1992). Similar structures are found in (9a) below, where adjectives again constitute arguments inherited by the head noun from its base verb. When there is no such argument structure, as in (9b), the range of possible interpretations snowballs.

(9)　(a)　electrical supply
　　　　　musical criticism
　　　　　dental treatment

　　(b)　electrical engineer, electrical shock, electrical generator, electrical clock
　　　　　musical interlude, musical comedy, musical composition, musical clock
　　　　　dental practitioner, dental appointment, dental care, dental floss
　　　　　medical care, medical condition, medical doctor, medical school

　　(c)　cardiac arrest
　　　　　friendly fire
　　　　　domestic goddess

Levi (1978: 52) argues for cases such as those in (9) that neither the head noun nor the modifier provides reliable guidance in such cases to the meaning of the AdjN as a whole. *Electrical* enters into a different semantic relationship with *engineer* from that with *clock*, whose semantic relationship with *musical* is in turn different from that with *electrical*. The range of possible interpretations of such constructions is determined by what we know about electricity, engineers, music and clocks. It would appear that the relationship of attribution provides the basic relationship of 'associated with . . .' in these cases; the specifics – for example that a musical clock makes music while an electrical clock doesn't make electricity but is powered by it – constitute encyclopedic knowledge, not linguistic knowledge. The objects denoted by such AdjNs cannot be identified without recourse to such encyclopedic knowledge. They are in that sense listed 'names' rather than 'descriptions' of objects.

AdjNs such as those in (9b.c) name specific things, a feature that is specifically present in the examples given in (9c): for various reasons, the basic attribution relationship does not even provide a general framework of interpretation for such forms, as it does in (9a). *Arrest* has a specific sense in *cardiac arrest* which does not obviously relate to the everyday sense. (That is probably why *cardiac juvenile arrest* is ill-formed.) Similarly *friendly fire* (already discussed) and *domestic goddess* are highly idiomatic – notably so beyond the idiomaticity of associativeness itself in such forms (compare *domestic animal*: 'tame, bred for agriculture'). Associative AdjNs have this in common with NNs, which have long been known to express highly idiosyncratic semantic relationships, such that the interpretations of *olive oil, engine oil, baby oil, hair oil; hair net, butterfly net, mosquito net* etc. are subject to encyclopedic knowledge (Downing 1977; Giegerich 2004, 2005b). Such knowledge is in a sense extra-linguistic, of course; but the fact that it is required for the interpretation of such constructions suggests that such constructions originate in the lexicon.

A more systematic treatment of the possible semantic relationships between attributes and heads, in the context of the putative lexicon–syntax divide, will be given in the final chapter. Here I conclude preliminarily that in associative AdjNs this relationship may range from the fully compositional 'associated with' via the expression of argument–predicate structure inherited from a predicate contained in the noun to the entirely idiosyncratic. The same range of interpretive possibilities is displayed by NNs as well as to some extent by ascriptive AdjNs, as we shall see.

I have shown in this section and the previous one that associative adjectives and AdjNs display a syndrome of properties which set them apart from their ascriptive counterparts. I summarise these here:

- Associative adjectives can be attributes but not predicates.
- Associative adjectives are not amenable to modification or gradation.
- Associative adjectives in many cases collocate only with arbitrarily restricted sets of heads.
- Associative adjectives cannot attach to heads already pre-modified by ascriptive adjectives.

- Associative AdjNs may display non-compositional semantic relationships among their elements.

These properties are at least consistent with an analysis whereby all associative AdjNs are formed in the lexicon. The generalisation ventured above whereby associative adjectives do not form adjective phrases accounts for their inability to form predicates or to undergo modification. But this generalisation may in turn be viewed as part of a bigger picture whereby associative adjectives are available for concatenation in the lexicon only, so as to form complex Ns rather than NPs. Phrases are formed in the syntax, not in the lexicon. And it is then unsurprising that, as lexical entities, some associative AdjNs collocate with less-than-full productivity – in the syntax, in contrast, we do not expect productivity gaps of the *vernal cabbage* kind – and that they can only occur 'inside' NPs as well as being prone to non-compositional semantics. Non-compositionality is associated with the lexicon in that such semantic behaviour occurs with some, but by no means with all, members of lexical categories: it is perfectly possible for a morphologically complex form to be semantically transparent. So, associative AdjNs are amenable to a lexical analysis.

However, that does not mean that the provenance of all associative AdjNs has to be lexical. As I discussed in detail above, most of the properties pointing towards lexical origin are also individually attested for certain adjectives known to concatenate in the syntax. Some AdjNs of syntactic origin do not translate into predicate constructions. Some other adjectives are not gradable and resist modification. The absence of *vernal cabbage* may be explained in other ways – perhaps this is a blocking effect in the syntax, exerted by lexical *spring cabbage* (Poser 1992). Sequencing restrictions in recursive attribution are also known in the syntax: *a German wealthy cousin*. While attribution in the syntax is by and large compositional, not all associative AdjNs have non-compositional semantics. And there is no reason to assume that all lexical constructions are semantically opaque.

On the evidence presented so far, then, all associative AdjNs are candidates for lexical status – a feature which sets them apart from ascriptive AdjNs. But this syndrome of properties does not enforce lexical status for all associative AdjNs. The remainder of this chapter will seek to establish the position of the lexicon–syntax divide in relation to associative AdjNs.

2.5 Associative adjectives and the pro-form *one*

Lexicalism holds that the elements of phrases are amenable to the operations of the syntax while the elements of words are not. We may therefore use the susceptibility of a given linguistic unit to syntactic operations as a test to determine whether that unit is a constituent of a syntactic structure or of a structure originating in the lexicon. For example, the elements of noun phrases – the only kind of phrase relevant to the present discussion – may be individually modified, such that in *long walk*, *long* and *walk* may be expanded into *very long* and *arduous walk* respectively: *very long walk*, *long arduous walk*. Syntactic modification is unavailable to the elements of both affixed and compound words: the adjectival base *kind* of the form *unkind* cannot be pre-modified (**un-very-kind*). Similarly in *bus driver*, *bus* is not amenable to phrase-level modification, for example by *air-conditioned* (**air-conditioned bus driver*), but modification of *bus* at word level – so as in turn to form a compound noun – is possible: *minibus driver*. This syntactic test for lexical status will prove useful in the discussion of NN constructions in the final chapter; but about associative AdjNs it tells us nothing that we do not already know from the previous section. Neither the associative adjective nor its head can take modifiers (bearing in mind the availability of recurrent associative attribution). I argued that this constraint is consistent with a lexical analysis of associative AdjNs but that it is also, possibly, amenable to alternative explanation.

A second syntactic test for phrasal status is the availability of pro-*one* anaphora, whereby the head of a noun phrase, if it is a count noun, may be replaced by the pro-form *one* (as in *a long walk and a short one*). Like the modification test, the pro-*one* test is commonly invoked to verify the lexical status of a given construction, under the lexicalist hypothesis and otherwise (Bauer 1998; Huddleston and Pullum 2002: 554 ff.). Pro-*one* anaphora is discussed in detail by Stirling and Huddleston (2002: 1511 ff.). Pro-*one* is unavailable to the heads of morphological units, be they nominal bases of prefixed constructions (**an entity and a non-one*), suffixes (**a writer and a read-one*) or heads of synthetic compounds: **a watch-maker and a clock one*. I will in what follows explore the applicability of pro-*one* to the heads of associative AdjNs.

Huddleston and Pullum (2002: 557) observe that associative adjectives 'mostly' lack the ability to modify *one*. Indeed, clear-cut grammaticality judgements are hard to come by; but informal queries with some ten native speakers revealed that there is a substantial number of associative adjectives that have no problems occurring in that position as long as suitable – that is, countable – head nouns are chosen. Consider the following examples:[1]

---

1. The grammaticality judgements associated with these examples were provided by ten departmental colleagues in a written survey. There is an urgent need for serious empirical work on pro-*one* before conclusions are drawn from its putative behaviour which are more finely grained than those presented in Chapter 5.

(10) (a) Is this the bovine strain of the disease or the feline one?
           Do you have a medical appointment or a dental one?
           Is he a rural policeman or an urban one?
           Is this a cold-water fish or a tropical one?

      (b) ?Do you mean the presidential murder or the papal one?
           ?Do you mean the parliamentary election or the presidential one?
           ?Have they made a junior appointment or a professorial one?
           ?Do you need a back massage or a cardiac one?
           ?Is this a subject review or an institutional one?

      (c) *Do you mean the autumnal equinox or the vernal one?
           *Is this the Home Office or the Foreign one?
           *Is he a constitutional lawyer or a criminal one?
           *Is he a theatrical critic or a musical one?
           *Is he an electrical engineer or an electronic one?
           *Is this a mental disorder or a nervous one?
           *Is he a financial advisor or a legal one?

Individuals may disagree with some of these judgments, as indeed the informants did among one another. The majority judgement was as indicated in (10): the forms in (10a) were regarded as uncontroversially grammatical, those in (10b) as questionable and those in (10c) as ungrammatical. However, some regarded all the data in (10) as ungrammatical while others accepted all of (10a.b) while finding (10c) merely 'odd'. But if this division of the data into three subsets – grammatical, questionable, ungrammatical – is at least roughly accurate then it raises serious questions regarding an analysis of all associative AdjNs as lexical entities. Under such an analysis, every one of the *one* constructions in (10) would constitute an anaphoric island violation, rendering all of (10) unequivocally ungrammatical.

If it is indeed the case that pro-*one* can never affect the elements of lexical constructions (and so far we have to take lexicalism's word for this) then the best we can conclude from the pro-*one* evidence is that there are speakers – namely those who rule out all of (10) – for whom all associative AdjNs are lexical. Recall that we have already confirmed the eligibility of associative AdjNs for lexical status on a variety of other grounds: under a syntactic analysis, every one of the features that make associative adjectives eligible for lexical status would have to be treated as a separate instance of exceptional behaviour within the syntax instead. And there are others for whom at least some associative AdjNs are produced in the syntax and hence eligible for pro-*one*. This first result, although perhaps to be expected, is important: different speakers may apply the lexicon–syntax divide, if it exists, in different ways.

If the judgements documented in (10) above are reliable then *a cardiac one* (= massage) is less likely to be acceptable than *a tropical one* (= fish), for example. This may be because cardiac massages and back massages are rather different procedures which cannot really be compared, or because *cardiac massage*, in common with the rest of (10b), has an argument–predicate structure which *tropical fish* lacks, and so the former is lexical while the latter may not be: again in common with the other examples in (10a), *tropical fish* is a straightforwardly attributive construction: 'fish associated with the tropics'. Recall here that such transparency makes a form eligible for syntactic status without barring it necessarily from the lexicon. We may also speculate here that the possible acceptability of *a tropical one* may be to do with the semantic instability of associativeness, discussed in section 2.2. It may well be the case that adjectives such as *tropical*, and perhaps others in (10a), are 'less associative' – and 'more ascriptive' – than, for example, *cardiac* or *papal*. The prediction would then be that *this fish is tropical* should be more likely to be acceptable than *this murder is papal*. This prediction may well be correct but clearly requires further empirical study (as indeed does much of what is suggested by the present, very small survey).

As for the link of the presence of argument structure with lexical status, there is a parallel here with NNs, which will be explored in more detail later: NNs with an argument–predicate structure are lexical (*watch-maker*, *basket-weaving*) while constructions such as *steel bridge*, lacking argument structure, may be syntactic or lexical (Giegerich 2004). If this reasoning is correct, if therefore all argument–predicate constructions are lexical, then why might anyone regard the pro-*one* data in (10b) as acceptable? I suggest the answer may be that all these examples are also interpretable in the more general attributive sense. A cardiac massage is a massage associated with the heart, a papal murder a murder pertaining in some way or another to the pope. Under that, less specific semantic interpretation – and compare a similarly 'blurred' analysis of *Tory leader* in Giegerich (2004: 19 f.) and in the next chapter – the examples in (10b) may be products of the syntax.

The examples in (10c) are not random either. *The vernal one* is ruled out because surely *vernal equinox*, with what for many speakers is probably the sole occurrence of *vernal* in English, must be lexically listed as a single unit. Similarly, *Foreign Office* must be lexical, but for different and perhaps more interesting reasons: *foreign* has a very common ascriptive interpretation (*foreign car*, *foreign student*) and a highly restricted associative interpretation: *Foreign Office*, *Foreign Secretary*, *Foreign Service*. Given the ambiguity of collocations such as *foreign office*, *the foreign one* is not ungrammatical in isolation (*Did you buy the British car or the foreign one?*); but it is odd in a zeugma-like collocation with an associative construction. Speakers who accept (10a.b) are unlikely to find (10c) worse than just 'odd'. All other examples in (10c) are subject to the same explanation based on the ambiguity of the adjectives in question. In collocation with *one*, associative adjectives which can default into ascription will do so; and when they have done so they collocate only uncomfortably with preceding associative AdjNs.

For speakers who do not impose a blanket ban on syntactic associative AdjNs, the reason for the oddness of *foreign one, criminal one* etc. is, then, that the collocation (in particular the preceding AdjN) giving rise to the pro-*one* construction requires the adjective to be associative, while the pro-*one* construction itself causes the ascriptive default interpretation and thereby a zeugma effect. For those speakers, *Foreign Office, criminal lawyer* must have lexical status if the assumption is correct whereby non-default interpretations of a given construction must be lexical while the syntax only provides default interpretations.

I return to this issue in the final chapter, as part of a more general re-evaluation of pro-*one* as a diagnostic for the lexicon–syntax divide. By then we will also know more about zeugma effects arising in the pro-*one* operation among associative attributes; and I will argue that it is those zeugma effects, rather than lexical status, which may inhibit pro-*one* – absurdly, it seems now, even among lexical constructions.

Two options seem to be emerging here for a lexicalist analysis of associative AdjNs. Either we assume a robust lexicon–syntax divide on the grounds of pro-*one*, as an example of the Lexical Integrity Principle. In that case the only apparent difficulty is that associative AdjNs somewhat misbehave by occurring on either side of the divide; and pro-*one* is producing results here which make it difficult to pinpoint the lexicon–syntax divide in the data. Or we assume that all associative AdjNs are robustly lexical for the reasons we have seen, while pro-*one* itself reaches into the lexicon, thereby falsifying the idea of a sharp lexicon–syntax divide in the sense of lexical integrity.

Note that the second option has severe consequences for our understanding of modularised grammars, but the first does not: it merely identifies a(nother) kind of construction which straddles the divide. As we saw in the preceding chapter, the transition from the lexicon to the syntax is characterised not only by a divide but also by some sort of continuum, however poorly understood. There is therefore nothing unusual about a given morphosyntactic phenomenon occurring in both modules, as long as it displays, whatever module it occurs in, the behavioural characteristics of that module.

The next section will take the search for evidence in support of either of these options one step further, awaiting a conclusion in the final chapter. For the moment, the question remains open.

2.6 The stress patterns of associative attribution

One diagnostic often invoked in the distinction between noun compounds and noun phrases is stress. Two-element compounds are said to have fore-stress, phrases end-stress (see e.g. Bloomfield 1933; Lees 1963; Marchand 1969; Liberman and Sproat 1992) – I noted this position and its problems in Chapter 1, and will return to it again in Chapter 3 below. This basic diagnostic works well in many well-known cases: *blackbird* vs. *black bird*, *whiteboard* vs. *white board*, *sweet-corn* vs. *sweet corn* – for more examples see Bauer (2004: 9). However, the situation is rather more complicated than these examples would suggest.

As I argued in Giegerich (2004) in relation to NNs, lexical constructions do not invariably have fore-stress. Consider the following pairs, whose members are semantically so similar that no case for a compound–phrase distinction accompanying the stress contrast can be made: *London Street* vs. *London Road*, *Christmas cake* vs. *Christmas pudding*, *town house* vs. *country house*. Especially in transparently ascriptive attribution of the *olive oil* type, which may be phrasal or lexical for all we know at this stage, variation in the stress pattern is common:

(11) (a) olive oil   (b) engine oil
           peanut oil   gearbox oil
           corn oil   hair oil
           sunflower oil   baby oil
           avocado oil   heating oil
           thistle oil   face oil

Although most of the culinary oils listed in (11a) will have fore-stress for most speakers, there is variation. *Olive oil* has end-stress for many speakers, and the rest are likely to follow suit in Scottish English (Giegerich 2004 and section 3.3.5 below) and sometimes elsewhere. On the other hand, the examples in (11b), displaying associative attribution rather than the straightforward 'made of' ascription of (11a), are fore-stressed. There is no variation among these. End-stress in *hair oil* would suggest 'oil made of hair', because the intended associative interpretation does not permit end-stress in such cases.

This is in line with the examples of NN stress doublets discussed under (4) above and repeated here: again, fore-stress goes with associative interpretations while end-stress implies ascription. *Toy factory* means 'factory for toys' if fore-stressed, and 'factory which is a toy' if end-stressed. There is no variation in what is clearly robust phonological knowledge on the part of the speaker.

(12)   toy factory
       steel warehouse
       hair net
       glass case
       driving instructor

We see, then, that NNs with associative attribution clearly favour
fore-stress; but under ascriptive attribution, stress patterns are at best
variable. These observations do not provide the complete picture – I
return to this question in the following chapter – but for present purposes they suffice in that they establish for NNs a clear link of associative
attribution with fore-stress.

If we assume, then, that end-stress is available both to lexical constructions and to syntactic constructions but that fore-stress is available in
the lexicon only, and if we also expect associative attribution to favour
fore-stress, then we may expect fore-stress to occur at least occasionally among associative AdjNs: either all or at least some such AdjNs are
lexical, as we have seen.

This expectation is met. Fore-stress is said to be somewhat less
common among associative AdjNs than it is among NNs (Liberman
and Sproat 1992), although it is not clear how such a claim is to be
quantified. It certainly is not unusual for associative AdjNs to have fore-
stress. I give some examples in (13) below, many of them from Olsen
(2000: 66):

(13)   polar bear, solar system, solar panel, tidal wave, medical profession,
       medical building, Medical Faculty, electrical worker, mental institution,
       mental hospital, mental disease, pharmaceutical company, dental care,
       dental treatment, dental appointment, circulatory system, legal work,
       legal advice, postal service, postal order, athletic department, financial
       advisor

There will be variation in stress in such cases, just as there is among
NNs such as *olive oil* and Bloomfield's (1933: 228) famous example
of *ice cream*. While under ascriptive interpretations (where those are
possible) there is invariable end-stress, as in *legal advice* (as opposed to
illegal advice), *dental fricative* (as opposed to *dental care*), we do not get
robust stress doublets driven by the ascriptive–associative contrast here
as we do in the comparable NNs in (12) above. The examples in (13) are
too variable to show such patterns; and in any case competing ascriptive
interpretations are available in a few cases only.

We will see in the next chapter that associative AdjNs are not unique
among AdjNs in allowing fore-stress. The point here is that any examples of associative AdjNs with fore-stress, such as those in (13), must be

lexical under the accounts presented by a long line of researchers from Marchand (1969) to Liberman and Sproat (1992), Olsen (2000) and Giegerich (2004): the fore-stress pattern does not permit otherwise. As we saw above, this is a reasonable prediction by the model for the specific data under discussion here, given especially the idiosyncratic semantic relationships displayed by some of the examples.

We saw in section 2.5 that an attempt to locate associative AdjNs in either the syntax or the lexicon is somewhat inconclusive. All associative AdjNs qualify for lexical status in terms of their distribution and behaviour, and such status would certainly explain their inability to head adjective phrases, and thereby also their stacking behaviour. But that does not mean they all have to have such status. If they did then we would be unable to explain why some, not all, associative AdjNs permit pro-*one*, a syntactic operation which, at least on current assumptions regarding the lexicon–syntax divide, is consistent only with syntactic provenance. Assuming an analysis whereby associative AdjNs strad- dle the lexicon–syntax divide seems to solve this problem. The results obtained so far prompt us to place the mechanisms which generate associative AdjNs in both modules, such that associative AdjNs which seem to resist the pro-*one* construction (e.g. *Foreign Office*) are lexical while syntactic associative AdjNs show no such resistance (for example *tropical fish*).

The assumption of a neat lexicon–syntax divide would moreover serve to predict point-blank that associative AdjNs which are eligible for the pro-*one* construction, and which are hence indisputably of syn- tactic origin, cannot have the (equally indisputably) lexical feature of fore-stress. Interestingly, this prediction is wrong.

In the sentences below, the attributive AdjNs from which the relevant pro-*one* forms are derived (*dental building, mental hospital, Medical Faculty, financial advisor, dental appointment*) are fore-stressed. This requires them to be of lexical origin. Nevertheless, there are native speak- ers for whom some or all of the sentences in (14) involving the pro-*one* construction are perfectly acceptable.

(14)   Is this the medical hospital or the dental one?
         Do you have a medical appointment or a dental one?
         Is this the general hospital or the mental one?
         Is this the Arts Faculty or the Medical one?
         Is he a legal advisor or a financial one?

This means that not only can associative AdjNs apparently originate variously in the lexicon and in the syntax; there are actually individual associative AdjNs (*dental building, mental hospital* etc.) which are simultaneously lexical entities ('compounds') with regard to their stress behaviour and syntactic entities ('phrases') where their attitude towards pro-*one* is concerned. This is a major problem for a theory which insists on neat modularisation: the evidence suggests that it is either the case that pro-*one* is available to certain lexical constructions, or that fore-stress is available to certain phrasal units. It certainly follows that the lexicon and the syntax are not separate, distinct modules in the grammar. They overlap in some way. I return to this problem, and a rather radical solution, in the final chapter.

Chapter 3

A *mythology of fore-stress, end-stress and tree geometry*

3.1 Introduction

I noted in Chapter 1 that stress is one of the criteria commonly invoked in drawing the distinction between lexical and phrasal constructions in English, for example between compound nouns and noun phrases such as *bláck-bird* vs. *black bírd*. Generalisations about English compound and phrasal stress have in fact attracted the interest of linguists for a great number of years, and this not just in pursuit of the elusive compound–phrase distinction: such generalisations have also been used to showcase a number of prominent elements of successive phonological theories, dating back to Bloomfield (1933), Trager and Smith (1951) and others of the era of American structuralist linguistics.

Trager and Smith (1951) used generalisations about compound and phrasal stress to demonstrate what they thought were the benefits of representing stress by means of an *n*-ary segmental feature assigned to vowels (while all other segmental features were assumed to be strictly binary). This representational sub-theory of American structuralist phonology resulted in a numerical notation of different levels of stress. The notation, if not the theory behind is, was subsequently adopted by early generative phonology (Chomsky and Halle 1968), and was to enjoy wide currency in stress-phonological research for another decade.

Chomsky and Halle, in turn, noted the property of the Compound and Phrasal ('Nuclear') Stress Rules whereby component stress patterns are preserved when they are embedded in larger constructions. This property was held to be a showpiece example of cyclic rule application, which was one of the most important and innovative formal devices on the derivational side of generative grammar. In phonology in particular, cyclicity was to become a central plank of generative formalism from the 'standard' model onwards (Chomsky and Halle 1968: 15 ff., 91 ff.; Halle and Keyser 1971: 15 ff.) until well into the era of lexical phonology (Kiparsky 1979, 1982; Halle and Mohanan 1985; Booij and Rubach 1987; Giegerich 1999), and indeed beyond.

43

In metrical phonology, a representationally oriented sub-theory within post-'standard' generative phonology particularly concerned with the relative prominence of phonological units, Trager and Smith's and Chomsky and Halle's *n*-ary stress feature was abandoned. What replaced it was an arboreal representation of phonological constituency structure and the expression of relative prominence relations within such structure (Rischel 1972; Liberman and Prince 1977). Notably, in this theory, the very same generalisations about compound and phrasal stress as those formulated by Chomsky and Halle (1968) were to figure, with much the same force, in an argument promoting a position exactly opposite to that maintained earlier by Chomsky and Halle: metrical phonology argued for *non*-numerical representation of stress, and indeed for *non*-cyclic rule application (at least in the domain relevant here):

(1)   (a)   Compound Stress Rule ('CSR'):
            In any pair of sister nodes [AB]$_L$, where L is a lexical category, B is strong iff it branches.

       (b)   Nuclear Stress Rule ('NSR'):
            In any pair of sister nodes [AB]$_P$, where P is a phrasal category, B is strong.

            (Liberman and Prince 1977: 257)

And subsequently, Hayes (1982) argued that Liberman and Prince's CSR supported his theory of extrametricality (in turn a sub-theory of metrical phonology), while Liberman and Sproat (1992: 147) at least regarded the predictions made by the formalism of the day as 'fairly well verified', reiterating an endorsement given earlier – if slightly more cautiously – by Kvam (1990), and confirmed by Kösling and Plag's (2009) more recent study of relevant corpus evidence.

The specifics of the structuralist, generative, metrical and extrametricality formalisms and their evolution are not at issue here, intriguing though they are, especially with the benefit of hindsight. Nor is the question of whether stress preservation effects observed in embedded structures really motivate cyclic rule application, or perhaps some more recent notational variant thereof (for example that of Halle and Vergnaud 1987, or Bermúdez-Otero and McMahon's 2006 notion of 'fake cyclicity'). For discussion of this particular issue see Collie (2008).

But what is very much of interest here is that all those theories' versions of the rules in question predict the compound and phrasal stress patterns presented in (2) and (3) below and, importantly, only those. All other stress patterns are therefore predicted not to occur. And not only the generalisations but in some cases even the examples themselves have been handed down from author to author, from theory to theory, and from the research literature to textbook treatments such as Giegerich (1992), Plag (2003) and many others.

(2)   Compound stress
    (a)   ŃN
           radio station
           community centre
           labour party

    (b)   [ŃN]N
           radio station manager
           oil-tanker driver
           kitchen towel rack ('rack for kitchen towels')

    (c)   N[ŃN]
           government working party
           university funding council
           kitchen towel rack ('towel rack in the kitchen')

    (d)   [ǸN][ŃN]
           labour party finance committee
           engine oil filler cap
           arts faculty entrance test

For phrases, the patterns in (3) below, end-stressed throughout, are predicted. Any non-final stress in such forms is held to indicate deliberate emphasis or contrast (*the néw book, not the óld one*), conditions of non-'normal' stress (I return to this concept below) under which any syllable in any string can receive stress.

(3)   Phrasal stress
    (a)   AdjŃ
           new book
           beautiful picture
           elementary proposal

    (b)   [AdvAdj]Ń
           very new book
           incredibly beautiful picture
           somewhat elementary proposal

    (c)   Adj[AdjŃ]
           nice new book
           large beautiful picture
           short elementary proposal

Note how (1) predicts the stress patterns of compounds to be distinct from those of phrases in all structural configurations shown: compare (2a) vs. (3a), (2b) vs. (3b), (2c) vs. (3c). Liberman and Prince's (1977) use of *iff* ('if and only if') rather than just *if* in the CSR, (1a) above, rules out point-blank the existence of compounds with stress patterns such as those in (3): all of those are characterised by stress on non-branching right-hand nodes.

However, the stress pattern of the phrases given in (3a) is also noted by some authors (for example Halle and Keyser 1971: 21; Zwicky 1986; Giegerich 1992: 257 f.; Plag 2003: 137 ff.) as occurring with certain 'exceptional' compounds such as those exemplified in (4) below. If such forms are indeed compound nouns and not noun phrases like those in (3a) – a question very much open at this point, but note that the examples chosen here are all 'names' and thereby prime candidates for lexical status – then the reliability of stress as a diagnostic in the compound–phrase distinction is in jeopardy.

(4)   Madison Road
       Waverley Station
       Brandenburg Concerto

Liberman and Prince's (1977) formulation of the CSR gave rise to the further, strikingly elegant claim that the prominence relations which hold among the elements of, for example, compound nouns are accounted for by the very same rule as are those holding, on a lower prosodic levels, within the metrical structure of non-compound nouns. CSR thus turned into the more general Lexical Category Prominence Rule ('LCPR'). Compare the stress patterns of, for example, *làbour party fínance committee* and *sèmolína*, *èxecútion*, both bracketed [[AB][CD]] on the word and foot levels respectively, where on both levels right-branching attracts the main stress. In contrast, non-branching right feet in *níghtingàle* and *pédigrèe* and non-right-branching compound structures (*ràdio station mànager*) put the main stress on the left. So, *all* prominence relations within a noun, compound or simple, are assigned by the same rule.

Liberman and Prince's LCPR is one of those highly valued but disturbingly rare examples of a major generalisation being visible only in, and by virtue of, a specific representational theory, and being masked by other notations. In the stress rules associated with numerical stress representations (Chomsky and Halle 1968), for example, the striking parallelism shown by LCPR had no way of being expressed. LCPR therefore represented one of the core arguments in favour of the representational theory of metrical phonology.

Moreover, like the 'exceptional' compounds not recognised by Liberman and Prince (1977), (4) above, non-compound nouns may sometimes, and clearly exceptionally (Giegerich 1992: ch. 7), have stress on a non-branching right-hand element – *bàmbóo, kàngaróo* and the like. So, in the vein of Liberman and Prince (1977) but going further than that account, we now notice that even the exceptions to the basic generalisation show parallel patterns.

And a further suggestion of a possible link between prominence and right-branching is provided by syllable weight, a phonological variable active in the stress systems of many languages including English (but not confined to the stress phonology): heavy ('bimoraic') syllables, favoured sites of word stress, are syllables with branching rhymes (Newman 1972; Allen 1973; Hyman 1977). Syllable onsets, left daughters of the syllable node, never participate in the mora count however complex they may be. Stress differences such as that between *agénda* and *América*, for example, are crucially linked to the fact that in the former, the penultimate syllable (*-gen-*) has a branching rhyme while in the latter it does not (*-ri-*).

So, the generalisations exemplified by the patterns in (2) and (3) are not merely well established in the phonological literature: they have also been of interest in a number of ways to phonological theory. And it seems that they form part of a larger, intriguing, yet poorly understood generalisation about phonological structure whereby at least in English, right-branching is linked with prominence whereas left-branching is not. This seems to happen among the elements of compound words, among the feet of non-compound words, within feet and even within syllables – a central generalisation in the suprasegmental phonology of English. Or so it would appear.

I shall argue in this chapter that at least where compounds and phrases are concerned, these generalisations, and with them the rules that have expressed them throughout the recent and not-so-recent history of phonological theory, are wrong on most counts. In particular I regret to have to show the following.

Firstly, while it is indeed very common for noun phrases to have end-stress, they sometimes have fore-stress, and this not just for reasons of emphasis or contrast – conditions under which, as I noted earlier, any stress rule can be freely over-ridden – but under well-defined semantic or pragmatic conditions relating to the relationship between modifier and head. I shall show this in section 3.2.

Secondly, as will be discussed in some detail in section 3.3, bipartite noun-plus-noun constructions ('NNs') may have fore-stress or end-stress, such that of the latter some are phrases and others are compounds violating CSR. There is nothing 'normal' about the patterns in (2a) and nothing inexplicable about those in (4) above: the 'exceptional' nature accorded to the latter in generative and metrical phonology was merely an artefact of a theory in its time unable to express their defining characteristics.

Thirdly, tripartite forms ('NNNs') – that is, NNs containing NNs as either their right-hand or their left-hand daughters – may have fore-stress or end-stress in both the embedding and the embedded NN. The patterns traditionally cited, and exemplified in (2b.c) above, are therefore not the only ones possible but a mere two out of a possible eight, all of which exist. This will be the topic of section 3.4.

3.2 The first myth: 'All phrases have end-stress'

Students of compounding are accustomed to the claim that compounds have fore-stress (with some authors allowing for the possibility of 'exceptional' end-stress, as in (3) above), while all phrases have end-stress – in particular those that keep figuring in discussions as to what is or what is not a compound noun: recall examples such as *gréen-house* vs. *green hóuse*. This is what (1) above predicts, as we saw, and what (2) to (4) exemplify. End-stress is thereby regarded as a sufficient condition for phrasal status and hence for the provenance of a given construction in the syntax rather than in the lexicon. It is not, however, a sufficient condition for syntactic provenance if compounds may have fore-stress or end-stress. (See also Halle and Keyser 1971; Olsen 2000; Giegerich 2004.)

The prediction of phrasal end-stress is expressed by the Nuclear Stress Rule of generative and subsequently metrical phonology (Chomsky and Halle 1968; Liberman and Prince 1977), stated in (1b) above; and, importantly, it is based on a more general (but not necessarily safe) assumption whereby there is such a thing as 'normal stress', the expectationof identifying one and only one 'normal', unmarked stress pattern for any given lexical or syntactic unit.

Essentially in line with this assumption, Dogil (1979) developed mechanisms in metrical phonology to assign non-normal 'emphatic' and 'contrastive' stress – the latter occurring in parallel constructions such as *déported, not éxported* – to express deliberate highlighting, as previously discussed by Bolinger (1972). Dogil's model reverses the generative assumption whereby phrasal stress is assigned by the Nuclear Stress Rule but may then be subject to synchronic shifting or reduction for the purpose of emphasis or contrast: under his account, emphatic or contrastive metrical nodes are identified first, and nuclear stress is assigned by a final (default) rule operating on any nodes not so marked. But the assumption that phrase-final stress is 'normal' is being retained in that account: Dogil merely modifies the technical interaction of its assignment with the treatment of contrast and emphasis. More importantly, his account has nothing to say about any non-final stress which is not driven by deliberate contrast or emphasis.

Schmerling (1976: 55–6) had previously dealt with examples such as those in (5) below, noting that both constitute 'normal' stress, but where

(5a) is more likely to be uttered in a pragmatic context recalling doctors, and (5b) in one recalling conversations.

(5)　(a)　This is the dóctor I was telling you about.
　　　(b)　This is the doctor I was télling you about.

Schmerling then argues that the generative model of stress assignment (Chomsky and Halle 1968), able to draw only on information encoded in the syntactic surface structure (in the sense of Chomsky 1965), is unable to distinguish the two versions of this sentence so as to predict two different stress patterns for it. This then leads her to abandon the notion of 'normal stress'.

Ladd (1980, 1984) discusses similar cases, but his account differs from Schmerling's in that it returns to the 'normal stress' assumption, proposing mechanisms which, in the synchronic derivation, de-stress constituents previously stressed by the Nuclear Stress Rule not providing information foci (in the sense of Halliday 1967). Thus in (6), the normal patterns *read bóoks* and *stand the mán* are subject to de-stressing so as to yield:

(6)　(a)　Has John read *Slaughterhouse-Five*? – No, John doesn't réad books.
　　　(b)　Have you talked to John recently? – No, I can't stánd the man.

Like Schmerling's examples in (5), Ladd's in (6) clearly do not imply any deliberate emphasis or contrast in the sense of Bolinger (1972) and Dogil (1979). For example, (6a) does not imply ... *but he burns them* (Ladd 1984: 255). What the examples do imply is the absence of focus on the nodes expected to receive 'normal' stress – *I was telling you about* (5a), *books* (6a) and *the man* (6b). These nodes are therefore subject to de-stressing. Notice that in (6a), the answer might instead have been *No, John doesn't read nóvels*, where a more information-rich final constituent might not be de-stressed. (For the link between stress and informativeness see also Bell and Plag 2012.)

Against this research background, consider now the two interpretations typically available to NPs such as *the well-prepared students*: 'those students who are well prepared (but not the others)' vs. 'the students, who incidentally are well prepared'. The source of such well-known ambiguities lies in the distinction between 'restrictive' and 'non-restrictive' modification, usually discussed in connection with relative clauses (as in the paraphrases given above) but also present in adjectival attributes (Jespersen 1924: ch. 8; Quirk et al. 1985: ch. 17; Ferris 1993: ch. 7; Pullum and Huddleston 2002: 554).

I showed in Chapter 1 that, unlike for example the distinction between ascriptive and associative modification (*severe decay* vs.

dental decay: Ferris 1993: ch. 2; Giegerich 2005a), the restrictive–non-restrictive distinction is neither directly nor indirectly encoded in the lexical semantics of the modifying adjective: non-restrictive modification arises unambiguously when the meaning of the adjective is part of the lexical semantics of the head, as in *the carnivorous lions*. Carnivorousness is part of the definition of *lion*: there are no herbivorous lions. But where the head's lexical semantics is unspecified for the meaning of the adjective, ambiguity will arise depending on whether or not the members of the set of entities denoted by the head happen – objectively or in the judgement of the speaker – all to have the property denoted by the modifier. If they do, then the adjective's interpretation is non-restrictive; if they do not, then the intersection of modifier and head is semantically more restricted than the head alone, and the modification has the 'restrictive' effect discussed here. Hence the ambiguity of *the well-prepared students*. If all students are assumed to be well prepared, then the modifier is non-restrictive; if they aren't, then it is restrictive.

I will demonstrate now that prosodic differences between restrictive and non-restrictive modification play an essential role in resolving ambiguity. Such prosodic differences, and concomitant differences in punctuation, are well attested where the distinction is made among relative clauses. When such ambiguity arises in adjectival modification, restrictiveness attracts stress to the adjective (Quirk et al. 1985: 1242). This stress is neither emphatic nor contrastive in the sense of Dogil (1979) – recall that contrastive stress is confined to parallel constructions (Bolinger 1972).

In (7) below, involving end-stress in the AdjN construction, the presence of the definite article makes a non-restrictive interpretation of *the well-prepared students* likely. Such a link between definiteness and restrictiveness was noted by Jespersen (1924: 111 f.), who observed that demonstrative determiners (which share an 'identifying' function with definiteness in general, as well as with restrictiveness) remove restrictiveness from following modifiers: 'In *this extremely sagacious young man*, *this* alone defines, the other adjuncts merely describe parenthetically, but in *he is an extremely sagacious man* the adjunct is restrictive' (Jespersen 1924: 112).

(7)　(a)　The well-prepared stúdents will finish the exam on time.
　　　(b)　The exam will suit the well-prepared stúdents.

But to enforce a restrictive interpretation in the presence of the definite article, stress must be placed on the attribute, as in (8a.b) below. On the other hand, in the absence of the article restrictive interpretations are likely regardless of where the stress falls: (8c–f). Indeed, stressing the attribute in such a context, as in (8e.f), appears to express restrictiveness rather emphatically, and redundantly: '*only* the well-prepared'.

(8) (a) The well-prepáred students will finish the exam on time.
     (b) The exam will suit the well-prepáred students.

     (c) Well-prepared stúdents will finish the exam on time.
     (d) The exam will suit well-prepared stúdents.

     (e) Well-prepáred students will finish the exam on time.
     (f) The exam will suit well-prepáred students.

The interpretations of (8a.b.e.f) are robustly restrictive. While the interpretations offered above for (7) and (8c.d) are less robust, I would claim that alternative interpretations will require more complex pragmatics, and will in that sense be less likely. If that is correct, then we may generalise that non-restrictive attributives have end-stress while restrictive attributives have fore-stress or end-stress. The function of fore-stress is to disambiguate in favour of restrictiveness where such disambiguation is necessary, as in (8a.b).

We confirm this analysis with a couple more examples. In (9), restrictive semantics is more likely than in (7) and (8):

(9) (a) The carnivorous ánimals don't eat grass.
     (b) The carnívorous animals don't eat grass.
     (c) Carnivorous ánimals don't eat grass.
     (d) Carnívorous animals don't eat grass.

Carnivorous animals can have a non-restrictive interpretation only where herbivores have been explicitly excluded from the discourse; hence (9a) is non-restrictive only in a context such as this: *This is the enclosure for felines. Note how overgrown the enclosure is: the carnivorous animals don't eat grass.* Examples (9b–d) are restrictive, identical to what we saw in (8).

The pattern shown in (7) to (9) is consistent with the ungrammaticality of (10b–d) below, where the non-restrictive interpretation of *carnivorous lions* – the only interpretation possible – is in conflict with, and effectively ruled out by, the stress pattern and probably also by the absence of definite determiners. (Mirroring (7a), a remote pragmatic context allowing (10c) may be available.)

(10) (a) The carnivorous líons don't eat grass.
      (b) *The carnívorous lions don't eat grass.
      (c) ?Carnivorous líons don't eat grass.
      (d) *Carnívorous lions don't eat grass.

What this means is that in restrictive AdjN phrases, fore-stress is available without implying any form of deliberate highlighting for emphasis or contrast. There is also no reason to believe that such fore-stress, associated with restrictive interpretations, is anything other than a form of 'normal stress': it is simply the stress pattern that goes with restrictive attributes preceded by *the* – recall (8a.b), (9b), (10b). If de-stressing is to be involved in the generation of this pattern, then this is in specific configurations obligatorily triggered by the adjective's restrictiveness in relation to (the lexical semantics of) its head, not by pragmatic conditions. As I noted above, cases such as (8e.f) are of a slightly different nature in that their fore-stress is redundant and deliberate, and arguably emphatic in the sense of Dogil (1979).

The analysis of phrasal fore-stress presented in this section (see also Giegerich 2012) – and in particular the observed link between fore-stress and restrictiveness – not only once more calls into question statements of the phrasal stress rule such as Chomsky and Halle's (1968) Nuclear Stress Rule and its successor in metrical phonology ((1b) above): this has been known since Schmerling (1976). It is of course technically possible within a powerful derivational theory such as generative phonology to derive one stress pattern from another, for example here the fore-stressed pattern available to restrictive modification from an end-stressed, 'normal' pattern. But the assumption that there must be for each phrase a single, identifiable 'normal' stress pattern is a myth; and the assumption of invariable end-stress at phrase level (in the absence of emphasis or contrast) is a sub-myth of the former.

More importantly for our purposes, the analysis presented here points to some unexpected parallels between the behaviour of phrases and that of compounds, which suggest that the findings presented here might have a direct bearing on our understanding of compound stress.

As we shall see in detail in section 3.3, compound AdjNs and NNs, just like phrasal AdjNs involving restrictive modification, may have fore-stress or end-stress. It is also the case, of course, that the modifying first elements of compound AdjNs and NNs are always restrictive: endocentric compounds are hyponyms of their heads such that a *blackbird* is a species of bird, a *textbook* a kind of book etc. It is impossible to conceive of a compound with a non-restrictive left element.

This means that there is a link between fore-stress and restrictiveness, to be observed at the phrase level but also present within lexical constructions (where the distribution of the two stress patterns is of course not dependent on pragmatic contexts, as in phrases, but arguably lexicalised with individual lexemes). I return to this issue in section 3.3.

It is also a matter of interest that in a lexicalist model, where the lexicon and the syntax are sharply distinct modules, it is not the case that fore-stress is restricted to the lexicon while the syntax knows only end-stress. The transition from the lexicon to the syntax is smoother than that: both patterns are found on both sides of the divide; and fore-stress under restrictive modification in the syntax is simply the postlexical equivalent of lexical fore-stress, comparable to a number of other well-attested cases of similarity among lexical and postlexical phonological phenomena (Mohanan 1986; Booij and Rubach 1987). It would have been surprising if such a postlexical equivalent of the phenomenon could not have been found.

Another interesting pattern is this. AdjNs involving associative adjectives are known to display variable stress patterns (*dental decáy* vs. *déntal hospital*) while, as we have just seen, AdjNs involving ascriptive modification (recall *well-prepared students* and *carnivorous animals*) do so only where that modification is also restrictive. Associative modification is invariably restrictive (Ferris 1993: 120 f.); and this fact may well be one of the reasons why associative modification so readily lexicalises with

modification, associative adjec-
ve) contexts where fore-stress is

further in the following sec-
t, in the light of the stress pat-
constructions, the dismissal as
stress identifies 'the important
nds (Faiß 1981: 134), whatever
mean, now seems a bit rash.

s or phrases?

Road etc., given in (4) above.
n actually be compound nouns
r whether they are simply noun
the latter position was probably
argued that *ice cream*, with its
ome speakers and a compound
re difference in meaning'. I show
iat within a certain class of NNs,
s is extremely common, so that
n type may in some dialects be

number of later analyses (for example by those of Marchand 1969, Liberman and Prince 1977 and Liberman and Sproat 1992), is simple and not unreasonable in principle: it is not unprecedented for a given construction to be lexical in one dialect and syntactic in another (see for example Laks 2013). But Bloomfield's analysis is compromised by an observation first made by Lees (1963: 120; see also Ladd 1984) whereby within the same dialect, *Madison Avenue* and *apple pie*, for example, have end-stress while *Madison Street*, *apple cake* – forms of identical syntactic behaviour and near-identical semantics – have fore-stress. Clearly, it makes little sense to say that in the same dialect, the former are members of a phrasal category and the latter lexical. It does make sense, however, to say it is possible for certain kinds of compounds to have the end-stress otherwise associated with phrases (Olsen 2000; Giegerich 1992, 2004).

The position opposite to Bloomfield's, whereby NN forms such as those in (4) above are not phrases with predictable end-stress but compounds with 'exceptional' end-stress (adopted for example by Halle and Keyser 1971: 21; Zwicky 1986; Giegerich 1992: 257 f.; Plag 2003: 137 ff.) – may have been encouraged by a simplistic assumption in early generative grammar whereby in the syntax, nouns cannot pre-modify nouns. All NN collocations must under that assumption be compounds – a position which survives in some recent treatments (Burton-Roberts 2011: 148; Olsen 2000), but not for example in Radford (1988) and Payne and Huddleston (2002).

But that position, too, is wrong. If *wooden bridge* is a phrase, as it certainly is, then so is *steel bridge* (Giegerich 2004: 7 f.). As I noted before, adjective-forming *-en* denoting 'made of' is fossilised and attaches to perhaps two nouns now – *wood* and *wool* – and with metaphorical senses to a few more: *silken voice* vs. *silk shirt*, similarly *gold(en)*, *lead(en)*. The derivational morphology of English no longer makes a productive process available to supply this kind of adjective (Marchand 1969: 270).

Nor does the morphology regularly procure denominal adjectives denoting places of origin other than countries – hence we find adjectival modifiers in *American car*, *British student* and noun modifiers in *London car*, *Edinburgh student*. I return to this important issue below, concluding here for the moment that it makes very little sense to say that forms such as *wooden bridge*, *British student* are phrases while *steel bridge*, *Edinburgh student* have to be compounds just because nouns cannot be phrasal modifiers (if indeed *steel* and *Edinburgh* are nouns in this context). It does make sense, however, to say that certain NNs may be phrases.

So, given that compounds may have end-stress, and that NNs may be phrases, it follows that in principle, end-stressed NNs may be of either phrasal or lexical (compound) status – a position long held in the mainstream of the Anglist literature (except Marchand 1969): Koziol (1937), Jespersen (1942), Faiß (1981), Bauer (1978, 1998), Giegerich (2004), Plag (2006), Plag et al. (2008), Bauer et al. (2013). This means that in the case of end-stressed NNs, criteria other than stress have to be invoked to determine whether they are compounds or phrases. I return to those when the distinction becomes relevant; for the moment it is not.

The reason why end-stressed compounds had to be treated as inexplicable exceptions in generative phonology – and see here especially comments by Schmerling (1976) and Zwicky (1986) – was at least in part an artefact of the theory. In that framework, the phonological component of the grammar interpreted a very simple syntactic surface structure, without access to any other, e.g. semantic, information (Chomsky 1965; Chomsky and Halle 1968). Crucially, that surface structure would not express the argument–predicate relationship present for example in fore-stressed *coach-driver, watch-maker* but absent in end-stressed *night rider, town crier*: the two types of forms would have identical surface structures. It was for that lack of formally accessible information that the theory was essentially unable to predict NN stress patterns: compounds have fore-stress except when they have end-stress. It would have been equally possible – and, given the unmarked nature of end-stress at the phrase level, perhaps even desirable under Occam's razor – to regard fore-stress among some compounds as 'exceptional' and end-stress as the norm across the board.

But there does seem to be a large residue of unpredictability in NN stress that goes beyond theory-specific limitations. Stress patterns such as *frúit salad* vs. *potato sálad* vs. *potáto soup*; *córn oil* vs. *olive óil* vs. *ólive branch* are known to occur, alongside various permutations, within single idiolects. This is not just a matter of (largely unresearched) dialect variation, although variation at that level is certain to occur as well. Examples such as these suggested to Schmerling (1971: 60 f.) that the stress pattern of a given NN may be driven by the head, or by the attribute, or by syntactic characteristics. I return to this issue below.

3.3.2 Fore-stress and end-stress in NNs

The overall pattern of stress patterns found in NNs is in reality far less chaotic than Schmerling (1971) and the formal phonological literature suggest: some important regularities, largely incapable of expression in the simple structural descriptions available to the rules of early generative phonology, have long been known.

We know, for example, that there is a class of mostly fossilised and syntactically irregular left-headed forms such as *procurator fiscal, court martial, chicken Kiev* and the like – the syntax of the English noun phrase cannot generate such forms – which despite their undoubted lexical status have end-stress. This is unsurprising given the French origin of this construction type, and given the more general availability of end-stress.

It is also known that exocentric NNs, such as *hatchback, air-head, red-neck* etc., invariably have fore-stress. Again, such forms must be lexical since their exocentricity is alien to the English noun phrase.

The subclass of NNs under consideration for end-stress also excludes NNs displaying an argument–predicate relationship, for example 'synthetic compounds' such as *watch-maker, coach-driver, train-spotter, dog owner* etc. (but not, for example, *town crier, night rider* and *boy actor*). Such forms have to be compounds as the relevant argument structure, as we saw in Chapter 1, cannot occur in syntactic attribute–head forms. They invariably have fore-stress (Liberman and Sproat 1992).

Bauer et al. (2013: 447) claim that this generalisation about the stress pattern of synthetic compounds is wrong, citing *party léader* as counter-evidence. In (11) below I give some more cases like that, consistently end-stressed by BBC newsreaders, in what appears to be an argument–predicate relationship identical to that in *watch-maker*. What Bauer et al. fail to note is that in these cases, the relationship between the two nouns is (also) amenable to an attribute–head interpretation (which may be associative or ascriptive); these are therefore not necessarily synthetic compounds (Giegerich 2004).

(11)   party leader
        Tory leader
        Labour leader
        Conservative leader
        Liberal leader
        world leader
        European leader

In such cases, encouraged perhaps by the possibility of a straightforwardly adjectival interpretation of *Conservative, Liberal* etc., which in any case is the only one available in *European*, the entire class seems to be amenable to interpretation as attribute–head. Note also that *world leader*, apparently denoting someone who leads the world, in reality means 'leader of global status'; and *global leader* (eligible for end-stress like *European leader*) is unambiguously an attribute–head form.

This reinterpretation of argument–predicate relationships as simple attribute–head relationships is probably encouraged by analogies (Bell and Plag 2012, 2013) as well as by the fact that many nouns such as *leader*, based on transitive verbs, are nevertheless available as free forms without complements in the morphology or the syntax. *Leader* does not require an argument; its dependent can therefore be interpreted as an attribute. The situation is different in the likes of *maker, monger, stealer, goer*, which are bound forms restricted to synthetic compounds such as *watch-maker, fish-monger, sheep-stealer, theatre-goer*. The first elements of such compounds are therefore never amenable to an interpretation as attributes, and end-stress is therefore never available to them.

A second possible reason for such reinterpretation is this. While the Tory leader is someone who leads the Tories, it is also true that he *is* a Tory himself, so that *Tory* may be interpreted either as the argument of *leader* in a synthetic compound, or as an ascriptive attribute to the head *leader*. It may well be that speakers regard the attribute–head interpretation as in some way the simpler one, and adopt it when it is available.

Kingdon (1958: 149 ff.) distinguishes between (a) NNs where 'both components are ordinary nouns', (b) NNs where 'the second noun is a *nomen agentis*' and (c) NNs where 'the second component is a gerund'. For category (a), of which for example *steel bridge*, *olive oil* would be members, he claims that 88 per cent of his data (whose origin is unclear) have end-stress, noting, however, that many nonce formations come into this category, and that 'a compound needs to become established before it tends to develop single stress [= fore-stress]' (p. 150).

For (b), of which *watch-maker* would be an example, he invariably finds fore-stress except where the first component is 'not the object of the second' (*town críer*). As we saw above, *Tory leader* is another possible example of this category. And for (c) he again has fore-stress in 88 per cent of all cases (e.g. *fóx-hunting*), the exceptions being items where 'the first component has an attributive function towards the gerund' (p. 153): *lead póisoning*, *mass méeting* etc.

Kingdon's statistics cannot be replicated now. More importantly, his reliance on 'established' compounds (and his implicit rejection of nonce formations as mere distortions of the picture) puts an undesirable bias on listed forms: it is actually the nonce formations that deserve empirical study. Much of the older literature, notably Marchand (1969), is guilty of this disregard of the productive aspect of compounding, focusing instead on the taxonomy of unproductive patterns such as *governor general*, *bird-brain* and *pickpocket*.

Nevertheless, Kingdon's categorisation reveals some interesting tendencies towards regularity. Note, however, that his categories (b) and (c) are both sub-categories of synthetic compounds characterised by the same argument structure; there seems no good reason to distinguish *nomina agentis* from gerunds within the category of synthetic compounds. On the other hand, Kingdon's category (a) where 'both components are ordinary nouns', and where there is stress variation, deserves far closer scrutiny than Kingdon gives it.

Fudge (1984: 144 ff.) states that end-stress among NNs (of Kingdon's category (a)) is likely to occur in the following categories: (a) where N_1 is a location or a time (*kitchen sínk*, *night wátchman*) and (b) where N_1 is a material N_2 is made of (*cotton dréss*, *meat píe*). Further categories attracting end-stress include *Ilkley Moor*, *William Smith*, *pound note* etc.

What is important to note here is that both Kingdon and Fudge identify NNs whose N_1 has some sort of attributive function as potential and perhaps likely cases of end-stress, while on the other hand items such as *watch-maker*, where N_1 is the 'object' of N_2 rather than its attribute, have fore-stress for Kingdon and are similarly not among the potential-end-stress categories for Fudge. These are fairly robust generalisations which, as we shall see below, also shed light on the stressing of well-known doublets such as *toy fáctory* vs. *tóy factory, glass cáse* vs. *gláss case, steel wárehouse* vs. *stéel warehouse* and the like. The stress differences in such doublets not only correlate very clearly with individual meaning differences (Faiß 1981; Ladd 1984; Bauer 1998; Carstairs-McCarthy 2002: ch. 6). Rather, as we saw in Chapter 2, they are linked to differences in the very nature of attribution.

There is, then, rather more pattern and less mess among NN stress than was assumed in the generative phonological literature. I want to argue in the next chapters that there is a specific subclass of NN forms which straddles the compound–phrase divide. Both fore-stress and end-stress may occur in this subclass; and while this is the only kind of endocentric right-headed NN in which end-stress is possible, its occurrence does not necessarily signal phrasal status. On the semantic side, such forms are characterised by a relationship of either ascriptive or associative attribution between the two Ns, though often their semantic detail is not fully derivable from the lexical semantics of their parts. On the syntactic side, they may be analysable into two separate domains by syntactic processes such as the 'pro-*one*' operation (Stirling and Huddleston 2002), or they may not be. I deal with non-phonological criteria invoked in the compound–phrase distinction in the following chapters; here I deal with stress in NNs without specifically focusing on the compound–phrase distinction among those.

3.3.3 *End-stressed NNs and the limits of formal prediction*

We are concerned in this section with the NN versions of the two basic types of attribute–head relationship exemplified with adjectival attributes in (12a.b) respectively:

(12) (a) beautiful picture
           blue book
           small elephant
           nervous person

      (b) musical director
           avian influenza
           vernal equinox
           nervous disorder

(c)   financial advisor
mental hospital
dental appointment
medical centre

Attribution in (12a) is ascriptive, ascribing to the head the property denoted by the adjective. This is the unmarked type of adjectival attribution, as already discussed in Chapter 1. In contrast, (12b.c) exemplify associative attribution: here, the adjective does not denote a property but – surprisingly for adjectives – an entity associated with the head (see Levi 1978; Ferris 1993; Payne and Huddleston 2002; again, this has already been discussed in Chapter 2). Thus, *financial advisor* is 'advisor associated with finance', *avian influenza* 'influenza associated with birds', *vernal equinox* 'equinox associated with spring', *nervous disorder* 'disorder associated with nerves'. I argued above and in Giegerich (2005a, 2009a) that for various reasons, associative attribution typically (but not invariably) occurs in lexical adjective–noun combinations while ascriptive attribution is usually associated with the syntax, although again not invariably so. Notably, adjective–noun combinations involving associative adjectives quite commonly have fore-stress, such as those in (12c), while ascriptive adjectives seem to trigger that pattern only in very obviously lexicalised cases (*White House, blackbird, greyhound* etc. – see e.g. Bauer 2004) as well as under certain pragmatic conditions involving restrictive modification (section 2.2 above).

Unsurprisingly, many such associative (entity-denoting) adjectives have ascriptive counterparts (for example *musical* and *nervous* in (12b)); and most have noun synonyms, so that the associative relationship is also displayed by the NNs in (13a). Example (13b) gives some examples of ascriptive NNs; *dvandva* compounds (Bauer 2008) are a subclass of NNs displaying ascription.

(13)   (a)   finance advisor
bird 'flu
spring equinox
nerve disorder

(b)   silk shirt
steel bridge
corn oil
toy train

(c)   singer-songwriter
fighter-bomber
boy actor
Alsace-Lorraine

There is no single rule for any dialect of English that might determine the distribution of the two available stress patterns within NNs such as those in (13), a distribution which is moreover subject to considerable dialect variation (and for that reason not recorded in (13)). In Scottish English more than anywhere else, end-stress is prevalent in such cases. Nor is this subclass of NNs sharply delineated. But I shall here propose the following generalisations.

Firstly, as we have already seen, the end-stress pattern occurs only in NNs displaying a straightforward attribute–head relationship. (I disregard the fact that end-stress is also found regularly in left-headed compounds such as *court martial* and *chicken Kiev* – this, as I argued above, has historic reasons unrelated to the compound–phrase blur discussed here.)

Secondly, end-stress favours transparent semantics over non-transparent semantics.

And thirdly, end-stress favours ascriptive attribution over associative attribution. In other words, the more phrase-like a given right-headed NN is, the more likely it is to have the stress pattern typically associated with phrases. I deal with these three points in turn.

3.3.4 Tendencies for end-stress: attribution, transparency, ascription

We saw above that synthetic compounds invariably have fore-stress, as in *watch-maker, coach-driver, basket-weaver* etc. Apparent counter-examples such as those in (11) are amenable to an alternative analysis involving attribution rather than the argument–predicate structure that characterises synthetic compounds: attribution favours end-stress.

Thus, Fudge (1984: 144 ff.) and similarly Kingdon (1958: 149 ff.) regarded end-stress as likely in NNs whose first element denotes time, place or material. Examples are given in (14):

(14) (a)   summer fruit
            morning coffee
            November rain
            Sunday timetable

      (b)   town crier
            London fog
            garden shed
            university exam

      (c)   steel bridge
            stone wall
            cotton dress
            meat pie

This kind of attribution is in many cases – e.g. in the material-denoting examples in (14c) – ascriptive; and certainly it is semantically straightforward and transparent, in the sense that the meaning can be comprehensively inferred from the attribute–head relationship and the meanings of its participants. Fruit associated with summer can be straightforwardly inferred to be fruit which grows in summer.

It is no coincidence that *leatherjacket* and *silver-fish*, both denoting insects, have fore-stress while their transparent counterparts denoting garments and fish, where meaning can be inferred, are usually end-stressed. End-stress favours transparent semantics. Similarly the forms in (15) below, where the contribution of 'milk' to the form's meaning is not transparent and the meaning of the whole cannot be inferred, unsurprisingly have fore-stress. These cases in particular will be revisited in Chapter 5.

(15)　milkman
　　　milk-fever
　　　milk-tooth
　　　milk-weed
　　　milk-float

Note, however, that end-stress does not absolutely require full transparency. End-stressed *village shop* does not just denote a shop located in a village, as one may infer, but in addition implies a certain range of merchandise. And not every house in the country is a *country hóuse*, just as not every house in a town is a *tówn house*. So, end-stressed forms may not be fully transparent; and fore-stressed forms such as *thistle oil* may be no less transparent than *olive oil*, which the same speaker may end-stress. It seems simply to be the case that, if such NNs are lexically listed as denoting, for example, particular architectural forms or culinary ingredients then they may or may not adopt fore-stress. The specific reasons why this may happen to a given form remain unclear; and a given stress pattern certainly does not seem to be predictable on formal criteria of any kind. Preference patterns may be driven by prosody, such that fore-stressed *town house* might fit a single foot while *country house* would not if it acquired fore-stress. Or they may be semantic, as Ladd (1984) implies when he observes that of all the possible street names involving, for example, *Madison – Madison Road, Madison Avenue, Madison Place, ...* – only the least marked, *street* in *Madison Street*, has fore-stress (also Bell and Plag 2013). Similarly, pastry names ending in *cake*, such as *Christmas cake*, less marked as a pastry name than for example *flan, tart, pie, pudding*, have fore-stress. (See also Lees 1963.) Frequency and analogy will also play their part, of course. See here in particular the various analyses found in Plag (2006, 2010), Plag et al. (2008).

While there clearly is evidence suggesting that in attribution, non-compositional semantics favours fore-stress while end-stress favours transparency, both features being more phrase-like, there is also a clear tendency for end-stress favouring ascriptive attribution while associativeness, as I first noted in Chapter 2, prefers fore-stress.

Firstly, consider the examples in (16) below, which show ascriptive attribution in (16a) and associative attribution in (16b), everything else being equal.

(16)   (a)   olive oil
               sunflower oil
               peanut oil
               walnut oil
               thistle oil
               avocado oil
               corn oil

        (b)   baby oil
               hair oil
               engine oil
               chain oil
               gearbox oil
               two-stroke oil
               anointing oil
               cooking oil

Dialect and perhaps other variation are rife among forms such as those in (15a) – most would have end-stress in Scots and Scottish English while in other varieties all may have fore-stress; or, inexplicably, *olive oil* might be the only example in (15a) to have end-stress. In contrast, the examples in (15b), all showing associative attribution, have no dialect variation. They are obligatorily fore-stressed.

This distribution of the two available stress patterns is shown with particular reliability in the doublets such as those familiar from Chapter 2 and first discussed by Faiß (1981):

(17)   toy factory
        steel warehouse
        metal separator
        hair net
        woman doctor
        glass case
        driving instructor

The pattern which recurs in any stress doublet one may find is that such a pair of forms is differentiated by the ascriptive–associative distinction, and that the former will have end-stress while the latter has fore-stress – indeed so reliable is the distinction that the meaning can be predicted from the stress and vice versa.

It may well be the case that some or all of the ascriptive versions of such doublets are phrases: it might be argued here that all that is exemplified by such doublets is the compound–phrase distinction, and that is essentially Faiß's (1981) view. But it is already clear that such an analysis would be flawed. The only thing that is clear and uncontroversial is that the fore-stressed versions of such doublets, and indeed fore-stressed NNs in general, are compound nouns. Associative attribution makes available for specific lexicalisation an unlimited range of non-inferable meanings (see e.g. Downing 1977; Fanselow 1981: 156 ff.; Olsen 2000; Adams 2001: 82 ff.), such that in (15) above a man is associated with milk in that he delivers it, a weed is associated with milk in that its sap resembles it, etc. Associative attribution simply has more room for specific, non-inferable (and in that sense non-transparent) interpretations than ascriptive attribution has. I will argue in the final chapter that associative attribution naturally gives rise to listing; and this connection in turn establishes a link in the present argument between associativeness and semantic non-compositionality as features in favour of fore-stress.

Decisive criteria for phrasal status would be absolute semantic transparency, as well as the separate availability of the individual Ns to syntactic operations such as pro-*one* (Stirling and Huddleston 2002; Giegerich 2009a). Hence, the compound status of *watch-maker* is confirmed by the ungrammaticality of **a clock-maker and a watch one*, and the phrasal status of *steel bridge* by the grammaticality of *a wooden bridge and a steel one*, for those speakers for whom this phrase is grammatical, and always assuming the pro-*one* is reliable in distinguishing compounds from phrases. Under this criterion, the end-stressed variants of (17) above would indeed be phrasal. But there is no reason to believe that all end-stressed NNs allow pro-*one*, and that they therefore have phrasal status on syntactic grounds. And, as we saw, the semantic criterion of transparency does not necessarily correlate with a given form's behaviour regarding stress; nor can we expect it to correlate with pro-*one*. I return to this issue in the final chapter.

To summarise, it is clearly the case that a more phrase-like NN is more likely to display end-stress than is one whose internal semantic structure is inconsistent with phrasal attribution. Fore-stress favours associative attribution over ascriptive attribution – the doublets in (17) above showed this quite clearly. In addition, and in both categories, end-stress is more likely with transparent semantics than in cases where the meaning of the compound cannot be transparently inferred. But there are no grounds for the claim that all end-stressed NNs are phrases (Bloomfield 1933; Marchand 1969; Liberman and Prince 1977; Liberman and Sproat 1992); nor is there reason to regard end-stressed compounds as 'exceptions' to a stress generalisation about compounds in general. End-stress is simply one of two possible stress patterns available to certain NN compounds.

3.3.5 *Compound stress in Scottish English*

To conclude this discussion of NN stress, I go into some more detail about the stressing of NNs in Scots and Scottish English. This will serve to demonstrate the sheer extent of dialect variation in NN stress patterns, and also to show how the semantic relationship between the two Ns is relevant to the distribution of stress in such forms. We will see here, I believe, a picture that is tidier in some respects than, but at the same time very closely related to, that of the Southern British variety described elsewhere in this chapter. Consider the following data. For a male speaker in his late sixties from the Scottish Borders, informally observed, the NNs in (18a) had end-stress, those in (18b) fore-stress:

(18)	(a)	horse shoe	(b)	bread shop
		Mars bar		paper shop
		post office		driving instructor
		bread roll		swimming-pool
		dough nut		oil can
		motor bike		timber lorry
		road end		
		salt water		
		sea water		

It is quite clear even from this small sample that all NNs in (18a) are of a straightforward attribute–head kind, where attribution may be ascriptive (*bread roll*) or associative (*post office*), similar to that in *steel bridge* and *country house* above. Indeed, one can imagine in all these cases a paraphrase using a real or imaginary adjective: *equine shoe, postal office, breaden roll, motorised bike, saline/marine water* etc. End-stress for this speaker appears to cover the whole range of NNs containing both ascriptive and associative attributes.

Note, however, that imposing end-stress on the examples in (18b) would result in unacceptable ascriptive interpretations such as 'a shop made of bread/paper', 'a pool that is afloat' etc. These items do not contain attributes of the kind found in the syntax, and adjective-plus-noun paraphrases seem inconceivable. Interestingly, a phrasal paraphrase would usually contain the preposition *for*: 'shop for bread' etc., signalling associative attribution in the presence of a potential ascriptive-associative ambiguity which is absent in the examples in (18a).

It would be tempting to conclude here that in (this variety of) Scots, all attribute–head NNs are basically treated as phrases – recall Bloomfield's (1933) assertion that *ice cream* is a phrase when end-stressed – while in Southern British English the cases in (18a) would be lexicalised, as evidenced by their fore-stress. But this would beg the question of why Scots should systematically fail to lexicalise such obvious candidates while other varieties of English do lexicalise them, so that such a conclusion would probably be wrong.

A more promising analysis is this. Given the ambiguity of NNs such as those in (18b), and given also the general unreliability of Scots stress in differentiating between ascription and association, as shown in (18a), the associative interpretations of (18b) are lexically listed. We may then further posit, in line with what we established in section 3.3.4, that these listed form–meaning pairings are listed on the form side with fore-stress. These listed, fore-stressed forms would then, in turn, block such associative interpretations for the potential, freely generated and end-stressed, rival forms. This is then a simple case of synonymy blocking, a device commonly deployed, and well expressed, in lexicalist models (Poser 1992), and one which is crucially linked with the presence of listed items in the blocking pattern (Giegerich 2001). This may then also explain why in the doublets of (17) above the stress contrast is so stable while in the absence of doublets, stress seems far more variable.

Moreover, Scots data such as these have to be seen in the context of a more general tendency towards end-stress in the same Scottish Borders and Lothian dialect area. The following place names from this area, all end-stressed by natives, are likely to be fore-stressed by Southern speakers:

(19)   Bonnyrigg
        Caddonfoot
        Clovenfords
        Dalkeith
        Lasswade
        Loanhead
        Newtongrange
        Walkerburn
        Prestonpans

... and many more, as well as of course *Newcástle* – like so many other 'Scots' phenomena, this may well be one associated more generally with Northern British English.

While many such place-names are historically compounds, they are of course by definition entirely lexicalised, notwithstanding their retention of end-stress. Examples such as those in (19) suggest two things. Firstly, the class of end-stressed nouns in (Borders and Lothian) Scots is much larger than its Standard English equivalent is; indeed, whether this class is 'exceptional' at all, as it is in Standard English (Giegerich 1992: ch. 7), must be determined by systematic research into the Scots stress system, none of which has ever been done. Jones (1997: 333) and Grant and Main Dixon (1921) report that at least in its recent history, Scots favoured end-stress for many nouns which in the modern language would not have end-stress. And secondly, the lexicalisation of semantically straightforward attribute–head NNs does not give rise to a tendency towards fore-stress in Scots in the way it appears to in Standard English. Indeed, if end-stress is not of exceptional status in Scots nouns then there is no pressure at all on lexicalised NNs to change their stress. There is therefore no reason to believe that the NNs in (18a) above were not lexicalised for that speaker. What counts here is the 'listing' of unpredictable interpretations, not the lexicalisation of linguistic forms.

This link between the stressing of compound and non-compound nouns appears to recommend a return to Liberman and Prince's (1977) generalisation, first discussed in section 3.1 above, whereby the prominence relations within compounds are accounted for by the same Lexical Category Prominence Rule ('LCPR') as are those holding, on a lower prosodic level, within the metrical structure of non-compound nouns: recall the primary stress on branching right feet in *sèmolína*, *èxecútion* and the secondary stress on non-right-branching *níghtingàle* as the regular pattern. If end-stress in *bàmbóo*, *kàngaróo* as well as in *Madison Róad* can be regarded as exceptional in non-Scottish but as quite regular in Scottish varieties of English, then the latter situation seems further to strengthen Liberman and Prince's 'LCPR' generalisation of a systematic parallelism between word-internal and compound-level stress patterns.

However, we will see in section 3.4 that Liberman and Prince's (1977) CSR, and with it LCPR, is flawed in that prominence relations among larger forms – for example [NN]N and N[NN] – are not in fact governed by tree geometry. All we can say is that in Scottish varieties of English, end-stress is less rare than it is elsewhere among both compound and non-compound nouns. Tree geometry may have little or nothing to contribute to an analysis of Scots stress.

3.4 The stress patterns of NNNs

3.4.1 *The myth and the facts*

Let us now assess the claim, expressed in Liberman and Prince's (1977) CSR given in (1) above, whereby the stress patterns of the two possible NNN constructions – NNs with NNs embedded either on the right or on the left, N[NN] and [NN]N respectively – are determined by structural geometry. A right-branching structure is said to stress the second N while a non-right-branching structure stresses the first: *kitchen [tówel rack]* vs. *[kítchen towel] rack*. As I noted in section 3.1, this was one of the show-case generalisations of metrical phonology, brilliant in its elegance and intriguing in its link between right-branching and prominence – a link which moreover seemed to be intriguingly recurrent in the stress phonology of English at both the syllable level and the word level. The examples first given in (2) above are repeated here:

(20)   Compound stress according to CSR
    (a)   ŃN
          radio station
          community centre
          labour party

    (b)   [ŃN]N
          radio station manager
          oil-tanker driver
          kitchen towel rack ('rack for kitchen towels')

    (c)   N[ŃN]
          government working party
          university funding council
          kitchen towel rack ('towel rack in the kitchen')

It is of course clear that the stress patterns predicted by CSR for NNNs exist: examples such as those in (20), as well as others cited in the literature from Chomsky and Halle (1968) to Liberman and Prince (1977) and Liberman and Sproat (1992), are compelling.

Similarly, in the first empirical investigation of its kind, Kösling and Plag (2009) found that in the Boston University Radio Speech Corpus (the reader will wish to work out the bracketing), the majority of NNNs overall conform to the CSR's predictions, although the CSR is also violated in a substantial number of cases. For example among [NN]N forms, end-stress is found to be quite common (*living room táble*). Sproat (1994) regards such forms as phrases containing NN attributes; whether this is a true explanation or one that is entirely circular depends on whether such forms can also be shown to be phrases on semantic and syntactic grounds, as we have seen.

I want to argue in this section that in spite of the existence of the two NNN stress patterns predicted by the CSR – and indeed of their relatively high frequency compared to alternative patterns – the generalisation expressed by the CSR is a myth, simply because every one of the other six possible stress patterns also exists. As a formal rule, CSR implies that anything it does not predict is ungrammatical, not just unusual. Its failure to predict all attested patterns will then render it wrong.

Every NNN is an NN with an NN embedded under its right or left node. As we saw in section 3.3, either of the two NNs contained in an NNN can have either end-stress or fore-stress, giving us four combinatory possibilities for each of N[NN] and [NN]N. I will show now that NNNs exemplifying each of these eight patterns can be found. Notably, we shall see not only that end-stressed forms can contain fore-stressed forms as one may expect, given the general expectation of more phrase-like patterns on the periphery of such a construction, but also that fore-stressed NNs can occasionally embed end-stressed NNs, thus proving the point whereby end-stress is available to lexical NNs. If, as we know, fore-stress indicates lexical status then any form embedded in a fore-stressed form must also be lexical. Clearly we are not simply dealing with some kind of lexicon–syntax 'continuum': if that were the case then no fore-stressed NN could embed an end-stressed NN.

We will see that the two stress relations occurring in each NNN are independent of each other, and that they are individually driven by the criteria discussed in section 3.3 above. Examples of each pattern are given in (21) below.[1] The two sets predicted by the CSR are shaded; the other six sets are predicted by the CSR to be non-existent.

The first point to be made about the NNNs displayed in (21) is that in each case, the stress patterns associated with both the embedded and the embedding NN follow the regularities described in section 3.3 above.

Firstly, the embedded NN has, in each case except (21bii), the same stress pattern as it would have in isolation. *Working party*, *sand-stone* as well as all other embedded NNs in (21a) are fore-stressed whether embedded or not. *Spring term* and *garden shed* as well as all other embedded NNs in (21bi) are end-stressed.

In (21bii), the possible adoption of fore-stress by those and other NNs under embedding – *spring term séminar* – is due to the more general eurhythmy phenomenon of 'iambic reversal', whereby for

---

1. All the examples in (21), with their stress patterns, were heard on BBC Radio Four and subsequently verified by at least three speakers of Southern British Standard English.

(21)

	(i) N[NN]	(ii) [NN]N
(a) *End-stress,* *embedded* *fore-stress*	gòvernment wórking party mòrning commúter train stèel wáre-house kìtchen tówel rack	sànd-stone wáll dèsk-top públishing lìving-room fúrniture bèet-root stéw
(b) End-stress, *embedded* *end-stress*	univèrsity spring térm alumìnium garden shéd plàstic toy tráin drèam family cár	sprìng term séminar gàrden shed róof sùmmer fruit púdding còuntry house gárden
(c) *Fore-stress,* *embedded* *fore-stress*	ówl nèst-box gráin stòre-room stéel wàre-house tomáto grèen-house	éngine-oil wàste óil-tanker drìver kítchen towel ràck stóre-room mànager
(d) *Fore-stress,* *embedded* *end-stress*	cóoking olive òil dessért ice-crèam síde fruit sàlad héating brown còal	garden shéd exhibition model ráilway enthusiast toy cár collection government commíttee member

example end-stressed *thìrtéen* reverses its stress pattern under embedding where a stronger stress follows, as in *thírtèen mén* (Liberman and Prince 1977; Giegerich 1992: 277 ff.). Those forms too are therefore entirely regular. No other forms in (21) answer the structural description that triggers iambic reversal; all preserve their stress pattern under embedding.

Secondly, the embedding NN in each case has the same stress pattern as it would have if it were not embedding, such that the stress pattern of an N[NN] is that which would also obtain between the N and the NN's head. The same is true for [NN]N; again, the embedding stress pattern is the same as that expected for only the NN's head modifying N. Thus, the embedding stress pattern in *government working party* is the same as that in *government party* or *government committee*. And similarly, *sand-stone wall* and *stone wall*, *university spring term* and *university term*, *garden shed roof* and *shed roof* etc.

So, whatever the regularities are that distribute fore-stress and end-stress among NNs, they operate independently in the two NNs contained in every NNN and determine that NNN's overall stress pattern. There does not seem to be a causal link between right-branching and prominence at all.

3.4.2 *Analysis 1: all end-stressed NNs are phrases*

Let us reconsider now an analysis, rejected in section 3.3 above, which treats all end-stressed NNs indiscriminately and as a matter of principle as phrases. This is the analysis originally proposed by Bloomfield (1933), and implied without discussion by Liberman and Prince (1977) and all other scholars who do not recognise the existence of 'exceptional' end-stressed NN compounds. Does this analysis save Liberman and Prince's CSR in the sense that it is able separately – presumably through NSR, (1b) above – to account for those patterns which the CSR fails to predict?

As we shall see, Liberman and Prince's NSR does account for some of those patterns, not all. But even that it cannot do without creating major new problems in addition to the one already identified in section 3.3 but here momentarily ignored for the sake of the argument – namely that on non-phonological grounds, some end-stressed NNs simply cannot be phrases but must be regarded as compound nouns.

Under this analysis, all of (21bi) and (21bii) would be phrases containing embedded phrasal NNs. Moreover, end-stressed *sand-stone wall* etc. (21aii) would be treated as a phrase in which a head noun is modified by an NN compound. Similarly, and notably, *government working party* etc. (21ai) should be analysed as phrases with NN compound heads. All these analyses are unproblematic as long as the phrase–compound distinctions within the forms in question can be independently motivated.

Note, however, that treating *government working party* as a phrase would entirely remove the motivation for having the 'right-strong-iff-branching' clause in the CSR, and with it the entire role of tree geometry, giving rise instead to a simpler CSR under which all compound NNs are simply fore-stressed regardless of branching. This in turn would legitimise the fore-stress pattern of *owl nest-box* etc. (21ci), which Liberman and Prince's CSR fails to predict, as well as agreeing with Liberman and Prince on the stress pattern of *engine-oil waste* etc. (21cii).

It is remarkable that this analysis, whose central assumption is actually shared by Liberman and Prince (1977), does not serve to maintain Liberman and Prince's branching-sensitive CSR but instead falsifies it. Nevertheless, and despite the damage it inflicts on CSR, this is a promising result where accounting for the patterns attested in (21) is concerned.

However, the analysis runs into trouble when attempting to deal with end-stressed NNs embedded in fore-stressed NNs (21d). Under Botha's (1983) 'No Phrase Constraint' and the more general 'Lexical Integrity Principle' (Lapointe 1980; Di Sciullo and Williams 1987; Scalise and Guevara 2005), syntactic phrases cannot be embedded in compound words. No NNN whose embedded NN has end-stress can be a compound if, as this analysis assumes, its embedded NN is a phrase. Example

(21d) gives instances of the two kinds of NNNs which embed end-stress under fore-stress.

Forms such as those in (21di) appear to be exceedingly rare. They are possible only where the embedded, end-stressed form shows clear signs of lexicalisation, thereby corroborating the Lexical Integrity Principle but contradicting the phrasal analysis of end-stressed NNs pursued in this section. Under such an analysis, the examples of (21di) are predicted to be ill-formed in that no compound can have a phrase-level constituent as its head. *Olive oil*, as we saw in section 3.3, is for many speakers the only culinary oil term to have end-stress: if fore-stressed *corn oil, peanut oil* etc. are compounds then surely so is *olive oil*. Note that *cooking corn oil* would presumably share the stress pattern of *owl nest-box* (21ci). *Fruit salad* similarly sits alongside salads which are fore-stressed (Schmerling 1971), and moreover varies like *olive oil* and *ice cream*. Adjective-plus-noun *brown coal* is a specific kind of soft coal ('lignite'); under a phrasal interpretation ('coal which is brown') this tripartite form would clearly be as ill-formed as **heating cheap coal* is. And in any case, if the end-stressed NNs embedded in (21di) were able in terms of their geometry to be simply phrases then we should expect a much freer distribution.

In contrast, left-branching forms with end-stressed embedded NNs – (21dii): *garden shed exhibition* etc. – appear to be more readily available although these, too, are ill-formed under lexical integrity if their embedded NNs are phrases. These forms are the NNN equivalents of a well-studied class of compounds which contain adjective-plus-noun phrases:

(22)   Lexical Integrity Principle
        open door policy
        affordable housing policy
        severe weather warning
        cold weather payment
        sexually transmitted disease clinic

There is widespread consensus in the literature (Carstairs-McCarthy 2002, 2005; Giegerich 2009a; Wiese 1996a) that the phrases contained in such forms are to a greater or lesser extent lexicalised, similarly to the embedded forms in apparent bracketing paradoxes such as *baroque flautist*: just as Spencer (1988) pointed out that *baroque flute* is lexical (compare *wooden flute* in **wooden flautist*), Carstairs-McCarthy (2002: 82) argues that phrases embedded in forms such as those in (22) are lexicalised or at least clichés.

However, under Liberman and Prince's assumptions the embedded end-stressed NNs in (21dii) cannot be of the same, lexical status as the embedded AdjN forms in (22); indeed even those forms are not predicted to be end-stressed by Liberman and Prince. They all violate lexical integrity in their analysis.

I return to the issue of phrases embedded in compounds in the final chapter, where this aspect of lexical integrity will be shown to be deeply flawed and largely untenable – though not for reasons which might be relevant here. Additionally, the problem just identified raises the question, once again, of what precisely is meant by lexicalisation, but here is not the place to go into this.

What is clear from this discussion is that Analysis 1, treating all end-stressed NNs as phrases, has the following consequences.

Firstly, Liberman and Prince's CSR loses all reference to tree geometry: this discussion has exposed a fatal internal contradiction in Liberman and Prince's (1977) account, which, as we saw above, actually shares the assumption made here in Analysis 1 (but not elsewhere in this chapter) that all end-stressed NNs are phrases.

Secondly, as we saw in section 3.3, if non-phonological criteria are invoked to draw the compound–phrase distinction then not all end-stressed NNs can be phrases: recall the observation whereby *country house* (which also occurs as an embedded NN in (21bii)) must be lexical on semantic grounds. It is wrong, then, to subject this form, and possibly others, to a stress rule whose input is phrasal.

Thirdly, the NNNs in (21d) remain unpredicted as long as we accept the Lexical Integrity Principle.

Analysis 1 is not viable, then. Bloomfield was wrong.

3.4.3 *Analyses 2 and 3: all NNs are or may be compounds*

Let us now reconsider an analysis, like the previous one also rejected above, whereby all NNs are compounds. If like Liberman and Prince (1977) we also deny the possibility of end-stress among NN compounds, then of course Liberman and Prince's (1977) CSR accounts for the examples in the two shaded boxes (21ai.cii) only, wrongly predicting the stress patterns in the other six boxes to be ungrammatical for various reasons. Examples (21aii.bi.bii) are predicted to be ungrammatical because they are end-stressed but, being NNs, cannot be phrases. Examples (21di.dii) are ruled out because they contain such end-stressed NNs, and (21ci) because the right-hand element branches without being stressed.

But we know already from section 3.1 above that for different reasons, an analysis treating all NNs as compounds cannot sustain the CSR in the form proposed by Liberman and Prince (1977): NNs may be end-stressed in the absence of right-hand branching; and to insist on them being compounds is to forego the convenient alternative, phrasal interpretation. This is of course why many analysts of that era allowed for 'exceptional' end-stressed compounds of the *Madison Road* type. So let us express the possibility of end-stressed compounds in a revised CSR, perhaps by changing the *iff* ('if and only if') in the CSR (1a) to *if* ('if but not only if'). This would predict the right-hand element of an NN to be strong if it branches as well as allowing it to be strong in the absence of branching (*Madison Road*). But a branching right-hand element could not be weak. In whatever way the old exception feature were to be encoded, it would allow 'exceptional' end-stress but not 'exceptional' fore-stress. This would leave (21ci.di) unaccounted for.

Moreover, like Analysis 1, Analysis 2 does not allow there to be a CSR based on structural geometry. In particular, the criterion of right-branching for cases such as *government working party* (21ai) is falsified by the presence of cases such as *owl nest-box* (21ci), of identical geometry but right-weak. Compare similarly *university spring term* (21bi) and *cooking olive oil* (21di), *sand-stone wall* (21aii) and *engine-oil waste* (21cii), *garden shed roof* (21bi) and *garden shed exhibition* (21dii). These stress contrasts are clearly not driven by tree geometry; what determines them is the regularities described in section 3.3.

Here, therefore, is Analysis 3. Recall that our initial reasons for the dismissal of Analysis 2 in section 3.1 did not relate to stress. Rather, the argument was that on non-stress grounds, many end-stressed NNs are clearly compounds while others must be phrases. *Wooden bridge* is a phrase; there is therefore no reason not to regard *steel bridge* as phrasal. We also noted that end-stressed forms such as *steel bridge* are often analysable by the syntax, such that for example *a wooden bridge and a steel one* is well-formed. So, subject entirely to criteria other than stress, end-stressed NNs may be compounds or phrases, if that distinction can be reliably drawn in all cases at all (which it probably cannot). This means that any one of the boxes in (21a.b) above may contain both embedding phrases and embedding compounds; certainly none of those stress patterns can be deemed to be restricted to phrases, or to compounds. Once again, CSR under-generates. (Note that row (21c) has no end-stress and is hence irrelevant here; and for (21d) we have already established compound status on the grounds of lexical integrity.)

This means that Analysis 3, more subtle in its treatment of end-stressed NNs than Analysis 1 ('all end-stressed NNs are phrases') and Analysis 2 ('all NNs are compounds'), does not improve the fate of Liberman and Prince's CSR either. In whatever way we draw the compound–phrase distinction on phonological or non-phonological grounds, in the light of the facts in (21) Liberman and Prince's CSR will not work. There simply is no CSR based on structural geometry.

On the other hand it does seem to be the case that the patterns predicted by the CSR are particularly frequent: Kösling and Plag's (2009) corpus sample shows this quite clearly. Why that should be the case is an intriguing but entirely open question. But the fact of the comparative rarity of the other six patterns, and even the possible absence of the pattern exemplified in (21di) from Kösling and Plag's (2009) corpus, tells us nothing about their grammaticality. Simply to call them 'exceptions to the CSR' would be to imply that they are not only rare but also in some sense formally defective, or irregular. As I showed above, they are not. A speaker who fore-stresses *síde salad* but end-stresses *fruit sálad* is likely also to say *síde fruit sàlad*. The occasion to do so may just not arise very often.

3.5 Conclusion

NNs in English may be right-strong or left-strong – on their own, under embedding, or containing embedded NNs. And while left-strong NNs are compounds, right-strong NNs may be compounds or phrases depending on non-phonological criteria. Expressed in a framework such as that of Liberman and Prince (1977), English therefore has two CSRs for NNs:

(23) (a) In any pair of sister nodes [AB]$_N$, A is strong.
      (b) In any pair of sister nodes [AB]$_N$, B is strong.

Without drawing up exact structural descriptions for these two rules, I showed in section 3.2 above that their distribution is far from random, and that it is driven by the nature of the dependent–head relationship in a given NN: straight attribution favours (23b) while an argument–predicate relationship such as that found in synthetic compounds requires (23a); and associative attribution and listed semantics at least favour (23a).

This not only means that the CSR accepted in the research and textbook literature for the past fifty or so years is wrong; it also means that an attractive generalisation noted by Liberman and Prince (1977) about a link between right-branching and prominence within lexical constructions is an illusion: I noted the apparent parallelism between *làbour party fínance committee* and *sèmolína* in section 3.1. But this is not surprising. The real parallelism is actually more interesting than the illusionary one in that it goes further.

As is well known, the Germanic subset of English nouns is characterised by fore-stress, with stress-neutral suffixation. To oversimplify only slightly, the metrical structures of Germanic nouns are left-strong throughout. Fore-stressed nouns such as *re-fit*, *driverlessness* etc. are clearly paralleled at the compound level by fore-stressed *nest-box*, *owl nest-box* or indeed longer forms, not here discussed, such as *barn-owl nest-box*, *nest-box maker* or perhaps *barn-owl nest-box maker*. Among the non-Germanic vocabulary, there is the set highlighted by Liberman and Prince (1977) – *sèmolína* etc., paralleled by *làbour party fínance committee* – but there is also, as I noted in section 3.1, a set of nouns which are end-stressed without being right-branching: *bàmbóo*, *kàngaróo* and the like. These are paralleled by *country hóuse* as well as the various end-stressed NNNs documented in (21) above. Recall also my observation whereby in Scots, end-stress is more common than in English in both compound and non-compound nouns.

What is interesting about English end-stressed non-compound nouns is that diachronically they have tended to abandon their end-stress in favour of fore-stress: this happened long ago to French loans such as *virtue* (end-stressed in Chaucer, like many other such words), and is under way in forms such as *magazine* (Giegerich 1992: ch. 7). The same tendency appears to be at work in end-stressed NNs, where lexicalisation and the (possibly diachronic) adoption of fore-stress seem to go together, if in ways which are poorly documented and not fully understood. While there is no discernible difference in behaviour between compounds with Germanic and non-Germanic elements, both the stress patterns and the diachronic tendencies within the language's etymological mix of nouns are paralleled in the stress mess of compound nouns.

Chapter 4

Interlude: the porous nature of lexical stratification

4.1 Introduction

Almost all of the discussion so far has involved the distinction between compound nouns and noun phrases. At times, the distinction has been stated in lexicalist terms, as constructions of 'lexical' vs. 'syntactic' origin respectively, thereby alluding to the lexicalist assumption of a modularised grammar. But in neither terminology has the distinction been fully in the focus of the discussion – all we seem to have learned is that it is a far from straightforward matter. Nor has the topic of the lexicalist modularisation of the grammar been addressed. This change of focus will take place now.

Under the lexicalist hypothesis in its basic, strong form originating with Chomsky (1970) and Halle (1973), the processes of the morphology, producing complex words, and the processes which construct phrase-level units constitute distinct modules of the grammar – the lexicon and the syntax respectively. Just as there is assumed to be a clear categorial distinction between words and phrases – for example between members of the categories N and NP – so is there held to be a robust divide between the two modules generating members of lexical and phrasal categories respectively. The presence of such a divide is crucial to the expression in the grammar of the 'Lexical Integrity Principle' (Lapointe 1980; Di Sciullo and Williams 1987; Scalise and Guevara 2005), whereby syntactic processes can manipulate members of lexical categories ('words') but not their morphological elements. This principle expresses the traditional view whereby words are the basic building blocks of syntactic structure; and it is of course entirely consistent with the equally traditional modular distinction between the derivational morphology and the syntax in linguistic structure.

Weaker forms of lexicalism have recognised that the inflectional morphology (Anderson 1982), or at least some of it (Booij 1996), applies in interaction with the syntax, such that the morphology mirrors the well-known distinction between lexical and postlexical phenomena drawn on the phonological side (Kiparsky 1982; Booij and Rubach 1987; Mohanan

1986). But such findings endanger the essence of the lexicalist hypothesis no more than does the recognition of lexical and postlexical phonologies; nor need the place of the inflectional morphology concern us here. What is important is the recognition that a given linguistic phenomenon, for example a phonological process or a morphosyntactic concatenation, can occur in a lexical and a postlexical version, thereby straddling the lexicon–syntax divide while in both of its modules of origin displaying the characteristics associated with that module.

Consider once more the well-known phenomenon of palatalisation (Mohanan 1986; Booij and Rubach 1987), first discussed in Chapter 1. Where this applies in the postlexical phonology, palatalising alveolar fricatives for example in *I miss you*, *I advise you*, it is a gradient and optional allophonic process, conditioned by speech style and other variables, whose application is not blocked by word boundaries and which knows no lexical exceptions. But where palatalisation applies lexically, as in *confess – confession*, *revise – revision*, it is restricted to word-internal contexts, where like all processes of the lexical phonology it is obligatory and categorical (though potentially subject to lexical exceptions), giving rise to 'phonemic' segmental distinctness. Characteristics such as these are associated not with an individual process but with the module itself in which that process applies, and expected to be shared by all the processes of a given module.

In the same vein, I shall in the next chapter scrutinise the AdjN and NN constructions since, under a lexicalist modularisation of the grammar, they too straddle the putative divide between the lexicon and the syntax. I will argue there that there is in fact no such 'divide' in the strict sense, certainly not one which neatly demarcates the point where in every respect and on every criterion one module ends and the next one begins: the facts of the compound–phrase 'distinction' are far more complicated than that. I shall attempt to account for those facts within a modular framework which postulates on independent grounds substantial overlap between the lexicon and the syntax.

To establish this framework, I shall identify a range of constructions which are simultaneously compounds in some and phrases in other respects. I shall argue that to do justice to such hybrid constructions, a formal grammar cannot have the sharp divide between the two modules that has been postulated in connection with the Lexical Integrity Principle. And hopefully, a formal grammar which thus recognises modular overlap will then also find it rather less difficult to deal with phenomena as elusive as lexicalisation.

We will see moreover that the lexicon–syntax divide is not only not a sharp one; it is also not unique, just as the lexicon and the syntax are not the only 'modules' in the grammar. The lexicon is not one module but several, usually called lexical 'strata' or 'levels'. We shall see in this chapter that the divide between those is no more robust than is the one which demarcates the syntax.

For reasons of exposition I shall set the stage for that final chapter by first looking at the topic of lexical stratification and its problems – an excursus which will, I hope, later shed light on this book's main topic, the lexicon–syntax 'divide'. I hope to demonstrate in this chapter that within the lexicon, the 'divide' between the strata shares many character-istics with that between the lexicon and the syntax, including its blurred nature: I shall argue that if lexical stratification is to model the facts adequately, then some overlap between strata has to be allowed. And if we recognise overlap between lexical strata then a number of problems, morphological, phonological and semantic, will fall into place that have proved recalcitrant under the original position of stratal integrity, which was shared by all research promoting lexical stratification (but see here critics of earlier stratification models, such as Aronoff and Sridhar 1987 and Szpyra 1989).

4.2 The nature of lexical strata

It is a largely independent sub-hypothesis of lexicalism – independent also in the sense that much of the criticism it has received makes no reference to lexicalism (Aronoff and Sridhar 1987; Szpyra 1989) – that the lexicon itself is not necessarily a single module but that it may be language-specifically divided into two or more ordered sub-modules or 'strata' (also known as 'lexical levels' – Kiparsky 1982; Mohanan 1986). A lexical stratum constitutes a domain for the interaction of specific morphological phe-nomena with specific phonological phenomena, the former in many cases providing the trigger context for the operation of the latter. In English, the domain of stratum 1 is the recursive morphological category Root, that of stratum 2 the recursive category Word, where the former is bound or free and lacks association with a lexical category, and the latter comprises free forms associated with lexical categories (N, V, Adj) – for details see Selkirk (1982) and Giegerich (1999: ch. 3). In such a 'base-driven' strati-fication model, a given affix may be confined to a single stratum or, as is frequently the case (Giegerich 1999: ch. 2), it may be available for attach-ment on both strata: I discuss an illustrative example later in this chapter. In the latter case, attachment on a given stratum will bring with it certain aspects of behaviour on both the morphological and the phonological side; those in turn then serve as diagnostics for the stratum-1 or stratum-2 provenance of a given morphological construction.

Before I outline those diagnostics of stratum 1 and stratum 2, I draw attention to one parallel between the lexicon–syntax divide and the stratal divide about to be scrutinised here. This parallel concerns the availability in principle of any given concatenation phenomenon on either side of the divide: just as, for instance, the concatenation of an adjective and a noun is available both in the syntax and in the final stratum of the lexicon, giving rise for example to *green house* and *green-house* respectively, so is, as we will see below, for example noun-forming *-er* available to produce both stratum-1 forms (complex roots: *manager, stenographer*) and stratum-2 forms (complex words such as *writer, singer*), in each case with all the properties associated with that particular stratal affiliation. Given this parallelism between word-level and morpheme-level concatenations, we have some cause to expect the relevant 'divides' themselves to have similar properties.

4.2.1 *Productivity and semantic transparency*

Stratum 2 is assumed to be the site of the productive derivational morphology of English: here are located processes such as the attachment of 'adverb'-forming *-ly*, of noun-forming *-ness*, adjective-forming *-less* and adjective-negating *un-*. Connected with the productivity of the process is the semantic – and, to be discussed below, phonological – transparency of the relationship between base and derivative (Aronoff 1976: 45): complex words such as *nicely, kindness, homeless, unpleasant* etc. are entirely transparent.

In contrast, stratum-1 forms are not the outcomes of productive morphological processes. Derivatives originating on this stratum are listed, perhaps because the morphological process behind them is no longer productive, perhaps because the semantic relationship between base and derivative is opaque or unpredictable. The former type is exemplified by *width, warmth* etc., where *-th*, forming abstract deadjectival nouns, is no longer productive – **weakth, *blackth* are unattested. As for the latter type, *-ity*, also usually in the business of forming abstract deadjectival nouns (such as *sincerity, chastity*), occasionally gives rise to derivatives denoting count nouns: *opportunity, fatality, fraternity*.

Much of the stratum-1 morphology is Latinate. Giving the listed nature of that morphology, this is unsurprising: it is rare for Latinate affixes to have any productivity in English. Moreover, the fact that speakers reliably implement the [± Latinate] constraint, which rules out the attachment of Latinate affixes to non-Latinate bases (**weakity, blackity*), can be explained only with reference to the essentially listed nature of that morphology. Speakers are not etymologists: Latinate affixes are simply not listed with non-Latinate bases. The [± Latinate] constraint, to which I return below, is therefore epiphenomenal to other features of the stratum.

I noted above that stratum 1 is root-based while stratum 2 is word-based. Thus, *-ise* attaches to some nouns (*victimise*) and some adjectives (*nationalise*) as well as to bound roots (*baptise*), so that the class of inputs to this stratum-1 suffix comprises both bound and free forms, and both morphologically simple and morphologically complex forms, while at the same time, the lexical category of the base has little importance in its selection. Similarly, adjective-forming *-al* goes with nouns (*institutional, autumnal*) and bound roots (*maternal*); and *-ity* attaches to adjectives (*formality, serenity*) and bound roots (*maternity*). I argue in Giegerich (1999: ch. 3) that all stratum-1 affixation bases should in fact be regarded as roots, even those which appear to have lexical category specifications (for example in *serenity*), and even those which are themselves complex (*nationalise*). The reason is, as we just saw, that every one of such apparently word-level bases can be substituted by a bound root. And bound roots cannot have lexical category specifications: if they did, then for example *matern-* would have to be an adjective in *maternity* and a noun in *maternal*, while the lexical category of *bapt-* would be indeterminately noun or adjective. Clearly, therefore, lexical category specifications play no part in the selection of affixation bases on stratum 1. The morphology of that stratum is simply listed.

The unitary base hypothesis, which asserts a crucial role of lexical categories in the selection of affixation bases (Aronoff 1976; Scalise 1984) may or may not be operative on stratum 2, where I assume the operation of productive morphological rules; but for stratum 1 the absence of such generalisations is in fact a defining characteristic. This confinement of the unitary base hypothesis to one specific stratum will then probably also alleviate the more general criticism raised against this hypothesis by Plag (2004) and Bauer et al. (2013: 635 f.).

4.2.2 *Phonological transparency*

Stratum 1 in English has a prolific structure-changing phonology, constrained by 'strict cyclicity' (Kiparsky 1982; Giegerich 1999: ch. 4), which stratum 2 almost completely lacks. Thus, stratum-1 derivatives are potentially subject to a number of phonological processes which result in various kinds of phonological distortion of the affixation base. Such distortion of the affixation base's phonological shape does not happen in stratum-2 derivational processes.

On stratum 1 are found the mechanisms which account for the various tense–lax and height discrepancies between the stressed vowels of base and derivative. In most cases these are synchronic residues of the great vowel shift, first formulated by Chomsky and Halle (1968: 178 ff.) and adapted to lexical phonology by McMahon (1990) and Giegerich (1999: chs 4 f.): *wide – width, serene – serenity, declare – declarative, Anderson – Andersonian* etc. Similar morpho-phonological alternations occur among consonants, for example in *electric – electricity – electrician*, or in clusters such as /mn/, reduced in *solemn* while preserved in *solemnity*. I discuss /mn/ simplification further below.

Moreover, stratum-1 derivatives are subject to the Structure Preservation Condition (Kiparsky 1982, 1985; Borowsky 1990), by virtue of which they are expected to behave phonotactically as though they were morphologically simple items. Thus, given that sonorant syllabicity is possible in English only on the right edges of words, base-final sonorants cannot be syllabic under stratum-1 affixation (*metre – metric, baptism – baptismal, kindle – kindling$_N$*) while on stratum 2, base-final syllabicity is retained: *metering, bottling, buttery* etc. – see again Giegerich (1999), as well as Mohanan (1986). And similarly, consonantal geminates, banned in morphologically simple forms, are tolerated only if they arise in stratum-2 processes: *keenness, soulless, vilely, night-time.* If in any such concatenative process a geminate is lost, as for example in *fully*, rhyming with *bully*, then this indicates a sporadic stratum-1 exponent of the process (unless it is a fast-speech phenomenon in the postlexical phonology).

Finally, the stratum-1 morphology interacts with the stress rules in such a way that right-to-left stress assignment, sensitive to syllable weight, is part of the stratum-1 phonology. Stratum-2 suffixes, on the other hand, are attached after, and are hence invisible to, the processes that assign word stress (Siegel 1979). As a result, stratum-2 affixation is stress-neutral, and stress-preserving: it leaves stress unaffected as in *ríde – ríder – ríderless – ríderlessness* etc. Stratum-1 affixation, on the other hand, is non-stress-preserving. Forms such as *atómic, solémnity* show no trace of the stress pattern associated independently with their bases: *átom, sólemn.* The stratal distinction in English in this respect expresses the boundary distinction – '+' vs. '#' – invoked by Chomsky and Halle (1968) to encode the difference between stress-non-neutral and stress-neutral suffixes, as in *+ity* vs. *#ness*, for example (Siegel 1979). But unlike that original boundary distinction, lexical stratification has a theory of morphology behind it.

So, at least in English, the stratum-1 phonology gives rise to a number of distortions of the affixation base: vowel changes (*divine – divinity*), consonant changes (*electric – electrician*), loss of sonorant syllabicity (*baptism – baptismal*), loss of geminates (*fully*), stress alternations (*solemn – solemnity*). At the same time, stratum-1 derivatives lack boundary signals (such as geminates): they are subject to the same phonotactic constraints as hold for morphologically simple forms.

Phonological distortion of affixation bases, such as that attendant on the stratum-1 morphology, has independently been shown to be linked to lack of morphological productivity (Anshen and Aronoff 1981; Hay 2002) – another feature of the morphology found on that stratum, as we saw. The parsing difficulties concomitant to the phonological opacity found in stratum-1 affixation are not shared by stratum-2 affixation, which is as transparent phonologically as it is semantically. Consequently, given the ordering of the strata, 'an affix which can be easily parsed out cannot occur inside an affix which can not' (Hay 2003: 23). Lexical stratification in this respect provides a formal model to predict the 'complexity-based ordering' of stacked affixes observed informally for example by Plag (2003: 174 ff.).

4.2.3 *Embedding and affix ordering*

Earlier models of lexical stratification placed considerable value on the 'Affix Ordering Generalisation' (Siegel 1979; Selkirk 1982). In such models (e.g. Kiparsky 1982; Mohanan 1986), every affix was said to be associated with exactly one stratum; therefore no 'stratum-1 affix' could occur outside a 'stratum-2 affix'. Given the recognition that it is not at all unusual for a given affix to resist such unambiguous association with a single stratum (Giegerich 1999: ch. 2), the Affix Ordering Generalisation is now as discredited as is the affix-driven stratification model on which it was based: while many textbook examples of ill-formed affix order (*homelessity* etc.) have been shown to be amenable to alternative explanation (e.g. Giegerich 1999: ch. 3), the basic fact that a given affix can occur on both strata has put paid in general terms to the diagnostic value of such instances of affix stacking failure.

Nevertheless, the serialism of lexical stratification does predicts that no form produced on stratum 2 can occur inside a form produced on stratum 1. The predictions of the model regarding stacking in individual lexemes merely cannot be generalised so as to hold for every occurrence of a given affix. Just as words (the recursive formal unit of stratum 2) contain roots, but roots (the recursive unit of stratum 1) cannot contain words, so too will formally or semantically distorted morphological constructions occur inside regular constructions (as for example in *metrically*, *fraternising* – stratum-2 suffixes underlined). Such serialism is enforced in the grammar by the Elsewhere Condition (Kiparsky 1982; Giegerich 2001). Similarly, the model predicts that phrases cannot occur inside words – but recall the problems of the compound–phrase distinction noted on several earlier occasions. Increasing domain size under embedding – roots embedded in words, words in phrases – corresponds then to increasing transparency of constructions, such that at the root level, complex forms may be entirely opaque (*fraternity*), as morphologically simple forms at any rate are, while at the phrase level they must be entirely transparent (*white board*).

Not only the behaviour of stratum-1 and stratum-2 forms under embedding but also, more importantly perhaps for present purposes, the availability of certain phonological processes, such as word stress assignment, to stratum 1 but not to stratum 2 represents a powerful argument in favour of lexical stratification – on each stratum, a specific morphology and a specific phonology apply in tandem. (See for example Booij 1994 or Giegerich 1999: ch. 1 for a summary of this key feature of the model.) Also, as I noted above, the phonological distortion attendant to the stratum-1 morphology is said to be linked to the lack of morphological productivity found on that stratum (Anshen and Aronoff 1981).

However, given that the stratal distinction draws on (at least) three different parameters – morphological productivity, semantic transparency and phonological transparency – we may expect forms to display a mixture of stratum-1 and stratum-2 characteristics. Such hybrids might arise, for example, if for some reason the base-distorting stratum-1 phonology affects a form which is otherwise the outcome of a productive process, and semantically transparent; or of course a formally regular complex word may lose its semantic transparency and require separate listing without simultaneously adopting other stratum-1 characteristics. Such 'lexicalisation' in the traditional sense of Lipka (1994) and Lipka et al. (2004), and notably distinct from a usage denoting transition from the syntax to the lexicon, is known diachronically to obscure the form or the meaning of morphologically complex words. In our terms, it represents the transition of a morphological form from stratum 2 to stratum 1. But a cause-and-effect relationship between phonological and semantic obscuration has not been and probably cannot be established: one can happen without the other. I hope to show below that to capture the effects of such gradual diachronic change in the synchronic grammar, that grammar must have overlapping lexical strata. I will then argue that once established in the grammar, modular overlap will offer new analyses, unavailable to proponents of stratal integrity, of some long-standing and recalcitrant problems. Let us first, however, exemplify the results obtained so far.

4.2.4 *An illustrative example: noun-forming -er*

Noun-forming *-er* may serve to illustrate just about all the characteristics of the stratification model of Giegerich (1999) that are relevant to the present discussion. I draw in this section on the descriptive accounts given in Marchand (1969) and Bauer et al. (2013), as well as on my earlier analysis in Giegerich (1999: ch. 2).

There is, first of all, no doubt of this suffix's presence on stratum 2: *-er* derives nouns denoting agents or devices from both Latinate and non-Latinate verbal bases; and it does so with full productivity: *singer, writer, speaker, lover, teacher, producer, commander* etc. are examples of agent nouns produced by this rule; *cooker, container, cutter* denote devices; *ruler, driver* denote both. In many cases the agent–device distinction is the outcome of blocking effects exerted by competing stratum-1 forms: a potential agent sense of *cooker*, for example, is blocked by the stratum-1 conversion product *cook*, while in *driller*, stratum-1 *drill* blocks the device sense (Kiparsky 1982; Giegerich 2001). But there are also a number of non-deverbal instances of *-er* nouns: *fiver, nutter, lifer, freighter, footballer, Londoner* etc., which, if Aronoff's (1976) unitary base hypothesis holds as a constraint on the fully productive morphological rules on stratum 2 and there enforces verbal bases for *-er*, must be listed and therefore stratum-1 forms. Their often unpredictable semantics would seem to support such an analysis.

I now present a number of examples of *-er* nouns which, for various reasons more important to our present purpose than Aronoff's hypothesis, must in the present model have stratum-1 origin. First consider the Latinate examples given in (1):

(1)   (a)   cartographer   (b)   professor
              astrologer   tutor
              astronomer   editor
              philosopher   investor
              presbyter   author

The list in (1a) gives examples of *-er* attaching to bases which must be roots, given their bound nature. Given that bound bases are unavailable on stratum 2, these forms must originate on stratum 1.

On stratum 1, *-er* has an allomorphic counterpart, *-or*, whose distribution among Latinate forms is essentially unpredictable, hence listed. The *-or* allomorph is distinct from *-er* in terms of orthography only, except where further, stress-non-neutral suffixation is available which causes it to be stressed and thereby to alternate with schwa, as in *professorial, tutorial, editorial* etc. Of the *-er* forms, *manager* is probably the only form available to stress-shifting *-ial* (*managerial*). And in a few instances, where it does not give rise to phonological alternation, the allomorphy is in free variation (*convenor/convener*).

The examples in (1) above, then, demonstrate a number of features associated with stratum 1. They are listed; they have an irregular distribution of allomorphs; and they are subject to random gaps: *managerial* vs. **philosopherial* and *tutorial* vs. **investorial*. They allow further stress-non-neutral affixes and must therefore, like those, themselves be attached on stratum 1 – an analysis confirmed by the fact that they are also available to bound roots. Yet they correspond to a perfectly productive and transparent, non-Latinate morphological process on stratum 2 which displays none of the characteristics of the Latinate stratum-1 forms discussed here. For earlier, affix-driven models of lexical stratification this behaviour and distribution of *-er* posed a serious problem (Bauer 1990); for the present, base-driven model it merely exemplifies what is expected.

I noted above that the stratal divide expresses the Latinate–non-Latinate distinction inasmuch as that distinction is of structural impact, but that stratification is not fully dependent on or driven by etymology. Of the three suffixes producing abstract nouns, *-th*, clearly Germanic in origin, is attached on stratum 1 like its Latinate competitor *-ity* (*width*, *divinity*) but unlike the productive process which attaches *-ness* to adjectives such as *good*, *kind* as well as Latinate *appropriate*, *ethnic* (where *ethnicness* is distinct semantically from *ethnicity*) etc. (Riddle 1985; Baeskow 2004, 2012; Arndt-Lappe 2014). The [±Latinate] constraint does not hold on stratum 2, nor is it a defining characteristic of stratum 1. In that light consider the following non-Latinate examples of *-er* attaching to bases containing final sonorants:

(2) (a) fiddler   (b) bottler
         smuggler   haggler
         settler   wriggler
         sprinkler   waddler

The examples in (2a) are likely to be bisyllabic, containing non-syllabic base-final sonorants, while all or most of those in (2b) probably contain base-final syllabic sonorants. As I showed in section 4.2.2, this discrepancy in behaviour can be accounted for by placing items such as those in (2b) on stratum 1, where base-final consonant syllabicity is routinely lost under embedding (recall *metric*, *baptismal*), while examples such as those in (2b), where the base remains undistorted under embedding, are produced on stratum 2. Indeed such an analysis has some measure of independent semantic support in some such cases: a sprinkler, for example, is not just anything that sprinkles but specifically a fire-safety or gardening device. A smuggler, on the other hand, is simply anyone who smuggles something.

This variation in consonant syllabicity is reminiscent of that found in *kindling* ('bits of wood used to start a fire') vs. the trisyllabic form *he is kindling the fire*. Chomsky and Halle (1968: 86) held the gerund (noun) vs. participle difference responsible for the phonological difference, positing a +*ing* distinct from a #*ing* (also Kiparsky 1982), but in the light of the syllabicity found in gerunds such as *the babbling of brooks, no loitering* etc., this cannot be the case. Instead, the difference seems to lie in 'lexicalisation' (Lipka 1994; Lipka et al. 2004) in the sense of a diachronic transition from stratum 2 to stratum 1, where semantic and phonological loss of transparency occur in tandem. But that leaves *smuggler*, with transparent semantics, unexplained.

I return to these examples later in this chapter. For the moment I conclude that lexical stratification can express phonological differences such as those among the examples in (2) by placing them on different strata, thereby appearing to predict links of such phonological features with the semantics.

4.3 Brackets and their erasure

In a stratified lexicon, the distinction between Chomsky and Halle's (1968) '+' and '#' boundaries corresponds by and large to the distinction between stratum 1 and stratum 2 respectively, and is therefore redundant. Kiparsky (1982) proposed replacing boundary symbols with structurally more expressive bracketing conventions, such that a prefix is lexically stored by a form '[X', a root by a form '[Y]' and a suffix by a form 'Z]'. Affixes and roots are concatenated so as to produce [[X[Y]] and [[Y]Z]] respectively, where the concatenation is expressed by an additional pair of brackets enclosing the concatenated elements. But, crucially, not all brackets survive all of the derivation (Kiparsky 1982; Giegerich 1999: ch. 2).

As I noted earlier, English has an alternation phenomenon in its lexical phonology whereby /mn/ clusters freely occur morpheme-medially (*gymnasium, omnibus*) and in stratum-1 affixation: *solemnity, hymnology, condemnation* (Mohanan 1986: 22; Giegerich 1999: 128 ff.), but are reduced to /m/ word-finally (*solemn, hymn, condemn*) and before stratum-2 suffixes (*solemnly, hymning, condemning*). This is another example of stratum-1 affixation bases being phonologically 'distorted' in comparison to stratum-2 bases, which are phonologically identical to their corresponding free forms: the stratum-1 base ends in /mn/ while its stratum-2 counterpart and the free form end in /m/.

We may account for these alternations by positing a stratum-2 rule which reduces the sequence '*mn*]' to '*m*]'. This correctly reduces the cluster in the stratum-2 form [[*solemn*]*ly*]] and in simple [*solemn*], and it distinguishes on that stratum between the configurations '*mn*]', '*m*]*n*' and bracketless '*mn*' (leaving the last two intact, as in *calmness* and *omnibus* respectively).

But given the rule's sensitivity to morphological bracketing, a device is needed in the derivation to ensure that complex forms such as [[*solemn* *ity*]], coming through from stratum 1 and containing morpheme-final '*mn*]', are not affected by the rule, just as morphologically simple forms with medial /mn/ (*omnibus*) are immune to it. Stratum-2 *mn*-simplification will produce the correct differentiation between stratum-1 and stratum-2 forms, applying to the latter but not to the former, only if brackets originating on stratum 1 are invisible to stratum-2 rules.

This device is the Bracket Erasure Convention ('BEC'), under which all but the outermost brackets of a given form are deleted at the point of transition from a given stratum. BEC thus ensures that forms such as [[*solemn*]*ity*]] enter stratum 2 without internal brackets: stratum-1 [[*solemn*]*ity*]] enters stratum 2 as [*solemnity*], where the absence of the internal bracket then serves to maintain the /mn/ cluster. Thanks to BEC, lexical strata are simply self-contained components insulated from each other: morphological complexity produced on stratum 1 is invisible on stratum 2, so that stratum-1 complex forms are, for the purposes of stratum 2, structurally non-distinct from morphologically simple forms. By the same token, all morphological complexity produced on stratum 2 in English becomes invisible at the point of a given form's transition into the syntax.

We shall see in the following sections that BEC is not without its own problems.

4.4 Overlapping strata: unexpected stress preservation and its unexpected failure

Recall from section 4.2.2 that stratum 2 is stress-preserving (*ríderless-ness*) while stratum 1 is non-stress-preserving (*solémnity*). These respective properties are part of the more general picture whereby stratum-1 derivation typically gives rise to phonological distortions of the affixation base, and thereby to impaired parsability, while stratum-2 derivation is fully productive, semantically and formally transparent and optimally parsable.

However, counterexamples to both have been noted in the literature, There appear to be cases where stratum-2 stress preservation ('strong stress preservation', as it preserves the main, 'strong' stress) fails. And there are cases where in polysyllabic stratum-1 forms the main stress of an embedded root seems unexpectedly to survive in the form of an otherwise inexplicable secondary ('weak') stress ('weak stress preservation'). I want to show in this section that both irregularities are amenable to explanation if we allow stratum 1 and stratum 2 to overlap. Moreover, both irregularities, apparently unrelated to each other, are then amenable to a single, unified explanation.

Burzio (1994: 247 ff.) notes a number of instances where, in terms of the lexical stratification model discussed here, stratum-2 forms display the stress behaviour associated with stratum 1 in that they fail to preserve the main stress of the base. I give some examples in (3b) below, next to their regular, stress-preserving counterparts given in (3a).

These examples have a number of things in common. Firstly, in each case both versions are equally grammatical: they appear to be in free variation. Secondly, they all have unequivocally stratum-2 suffixation. Thirdly, they have primary stress as on the penultimate syllable where that syllable is heavy (*dòcuménted*) and on the antepenultimate syllable where the penult is light (*èlementárily*). Fourthly, they have a secondary stress on the first syllable. And fifthly, these non-stress-preserving forms are synonymous with their stress-preserving counterparts in (3a): their semantics shows no signs of lexicalisation of the kind observed in connection with *kindling, sprinkler* etc. in section 4.2.2 above.

(3) (a) eleméntary – eleméntarily   (b) èlementárily
          nécessary – nécessarily   nècessárily
          compleméntary – compleméntarily   còmplementárily
          órdinary – órdinarily   òrdinárily
          dócument$_V$ – dócumented   dòcuménted
          dócument$_V$ – dócumenting   dòcuménting
          árbitrary – árbitrariness   àrbitráriness

Note that the stress pattern shared by the forms in (3b) is itself not strictly speaking irregular: it is merely that of the 'wrong' stratum. Under a stratum-1 stress regime of right-to-left main stress assignment, all the forms in (3b) would be entirely regular. The examples in (3b) and (3a) simply reflect the stress patterns predicted for such forms by the lexical phonologies of stratum 1 and stratum 2 respectively. The problem is merely that they are not stratum-1 forms.

Of course the base-driven stratification model, where a given affix is not confined to a single stratum, would permit us to assign such forms individually to stratum 1 purely on the grounds of their phonological behaviour, even though *-ly*, *-ness* etc. are fully productive on stratum 2. We saw this in the preceding section in connection with noun-forming *-er*. But such a solution, amounting to a treatment of such forms as individually listed in the lexicon, is implausible. There is no reason other than phonological for such listing – no semantic opacity, for example, that would set such forms apart from their equally common stress-preserving alternatives (*eleméntarily* etc.). This is just speaker-specific variation in stress. Moreover, these forms constitute a reasonably well-defined set, as we shall see.

What seems to drive this preservation failure and the adoption instead of the Latinate stratum-1 pattern is the Latinacy of the base itself, paired perhaps with the large number of syllables following the stress of the base. Certainly, the phenomenon seems to affect all forms ending in *-arily* and *-ariness*. But in the present model no explanation arises from this observation. Firstly, Latinacy is an accidental characteristic, not a defining characteristic, of stratum 1. Secondly, any possible suggestion that *-arily* might be some fused suffix combination located on stratum 1 is not helpful either, given that the phenomenon also occurs with *-ed* and *-ing*. What we have here is simply stratum-1–like stress behaviour on the part of an identifiable set of stratum-2 forms. This means that the stratum-1 stress phonology – weight-sensitive right-to-left assignment – is available to, and hence overlaps with, some of the stratum-2 morphology. I continue the analysis of these cases further below in this section. Let us first turn to weak stress preservation – that is, the preservation of embedded secondary stress unexpectedly occurring in stratum-1 affixation bases.

It is one of the lesser-known regularities of English stress that words cannot begin with two or more entirely unstressed syllables, followed by the main stress. One of those syllables will bear a secondary stress. Where two syllables precede the main stress, the secondary stress will fall on the first (*ìntrodúctory, còntribútion*), but in the case of three or more such syllables, either of the first two is available. Kiparsky (1979) observed different placement of secondary stresses in morphologically complex forms such as *sensàtionálity* and underived forms such as *Tìconderóga*, and claimed on that basis that weak stress preservation is the norm on (what the present model refers to as) stratum 1. Stress assignment in stratum-1 complex forms, he argued, must therefore be cyclic.

However, more recent work by Collie (2008) has shown that the empirical validity of Kiparsky's claim is highly doubtful: secondary stress in monomorphemic words is in fact highly variable, as exemplified in (4a) below. And so is, in many cases, secondary stress in stratum-1 derivatives: (4b.c). The behaviour of the two sets is therefore not really as systematically distinct as Kiparsky believed; and the case for weak preservation, and hence for the cyclicity of stratum-1 stress assignment, is itself weak.

(4)   (a)   Còriolánus ~ Corìolánus
              Lòuisiána ~ Louìsiána
              Tìconderóga ~ Ticònderóga

       (b)   èxperiméntal
              cò-operátion
              ìllegibílity

       (c)   expèriméntal   (expériment)
              co-òperátion   (co-óperate)
              illègibílity   (illégible)

Drawing on Selkirk's (1980) templatic approach to word stress, Collie proposes the generalisation whereby in monomorphemic cases such as those in (4a), secondary stress on either of the first two syllables is well-formed so long as a light syllable is not selected in preference over a neighbouring heavy syllable. In the examples, the first two syllables are of equal weight – both are light in *Coriolanus* and both heavy in the other two.

The same generalisation then also accounts for the initially stressed (non-stress-preserving) variants of stratum-1 complex forms in (4b). But that generalisation leaves the variants given in (4c), with secondary stress on light second syllables following a heavy first syllable, unexplained.

However, given the identity of the embedded pattern with that of the corresponding free forms in these cases, they do seem to be consistent with weak stress preservation among stratum-1 forms and thereby constitute a small measure of evidence for this phenomenon. Curiously, this sporadic preservation seems to be just as optional as the sporadic failure of strong preservation discussed under (3) above. Again, stratal overlap offers a solution.

We have now come across two separate mechanisms for the assignment of stress. The first rule, Latinate in origin (Halle and Keyser 1971; Hyman 1977) assigns stress to the penultimate syllable if that syllable is heavy, otherwise to the antepenult. This stress, applied right-to-left, usually ends up as the word's primary stress. The second rule, shown by Collie (2008) also to be weight-sensitive, assigns stress left-to-right and results in a secondary stress on one of the two first syllables.

There is ample evidence suggesting that right-to-left, weight-sensitive stress assignment Latin-style is associated with stratum 1: this stratal affiliation accounts both for stratum-1 non-stress-neutrality, as in *sólemn – solémnity*, and for stratum-2 *ríderlessness*, where the three derivational suffixes attached to *ride* are stress-neutral. But there is no reason to insist that the left-to-right assignment of stress, rhythmically motivated and similarly favouring heavy syllables, also happens on stratum 1. Indeed, the fact that stratum-2 prefixes are available to such stress (*ùnpredíctable, rè-assígn*), and therefore have to be present when the stress rule applies, can only be accounted for by positing that stress rule on stratum 2.

Let us assume that the two mechanisms simply assign stress, not differentiating at the point of assignment between primary and secondary stress. This then means that all the examples in (4) and, under the provision of stratal overlap, those in (3) receive their right-hand stress through the stratum-1 mechanisms while the left-hand stresses in (3) and (4a.b) are provided on stratum 2.

For the cases of weak stress preservation in (4c) – *expèriméntal* etc. – two options then seem to be available. The first of these involves reintroducing cyclic stress assignment into stratum-1 stress as a non-obligatory device. This would then pre-empt application of the stratum-2 left-to-right stress rule: there would not be a sequence of unstressed syllables for that rule to operate on. But, clearly, introducing even 'optional' cyclicity would be against the spirit of phonological and semantic opacity prevalent on stratum 1; it would come at a heavy cost in terms of the complexity of the grammar; and it would in any case be unavailable to optimality-theoretic accounts of the phenomenon even in versions of stratal OT as developed by Kiparsky (2000) and Bermúdez-Otero (2003). This option clearly has to be disfavoured.

The second option is to regard the weak 'preservation' effect as an illusion. This effect only ever occurs on the first or second syllable:

English does not allow word-initial sequences of unstressed syllables. There is then no reason to insist that this stress is the derivational residue of earlier right-to-left assignment of stress to an embedded form. It may as well be the result of independent stratum-2 left-to-right assignment, as it is in any case in *Ticònderóga*.

The reason why, exceptionally, a light syllable may be preferred over an initial heavy syllable in such cases is then simply that under stratal overlap, the embedded form *experiment* is still structurally visible at the point of left-to-right stress assignment on stratum 2, as in [[*experiment*] *al*]. In the normal case we would expect internal brackets to have been deleted, by virtue of the Bracket Erasure Convention, in the transition from stratum 1 to stratum 2 (see Kiparsky 1982; Giegerich 1999: 9; and section 4.3 above), giving [*experimental*] the same (non-)complexity where stratum-2 processes are concerned as [*Ticonderoga*].

Speakers then put that stress in *experiment(al)* where in the corresponding, listed stratum-1 item *experiment* they would expect it to fall. In effect this means the optional retention of the form's internal bracketing. This dependence of stress assignment on the recognition of the embedded form accounts very straightforwardly for the haphazard nature of weak 'preservation' – no recognition, no preservation – and in fact links its occurrence to high relative frequency, causing a high likelihood of recognition, of the base (Collie 2008). Moreover the deployment of a stratum-2 device is consistent with the assumption of opacity that characterises the phonology of stratum 1. Note finally that dealing with the weak preservation effect in the stratal overlap area of the lexicon will then leave the straightforward left-to-right stressing, in (3), (4a) and the non-preserving variants of (4b), as the mainstream stratum-2 default. It is only in the non-default cases which show weak stress preservation that stratum-2 stress can work on a stratum-1 structure.

I suggested above that stresses assigned right-to-left and left-to-right are equal in 'strength' at the point of assignment. This is neither controversial nor dependent on the representational devices used. A unified account of strong stress preservation failure and weak 'preservation' depends on the simple assumption that the contouring of stresses – such that in all the cases observed above the left-hand stress is secondary to the right-hand stress – is a separate matter.

For two independent reasons, this contouring of stresses can take place as late as on stratum 2. Firstly, contoured stress is not needed on stratum 1: while the difference between stress being present or absent counts for example in the phonotactics of vowels (Giegerich 1992: 66 ff.), there are no phonological processes on stratum 1 which need to refer to the difference between primary and secondary stress. And secondly, as Liberman and Prince (1977) were the first to point out, the mechanism providing contours of secondary and primary stresses in words (Liberman and

Prince's 'Lexical Category Prominence Rule') is related to – although, as we saw in the preceding chapter, not nearly as closely as they originally claimed – the mechanism responsible for the stress contours of compounds, including the fore-stress pattern of two-element compounds. And as we know, compounds are the products of stratum 2. So, my suggestion that left-to-right stress assignment takes place on stratum 2 so as to include certain prefixes in its domain (recall *ùnpredíctable*, *rè-assígn*) is consistent with the rest of the stress phonology relevant here.

The finer details of stress preservation and its possible failure in English clearly suggest overlap of lexical strata. Such a model finds it easy to account for stratum-2 forms adopting stratum-1 phonological behaviour, and it makes reasonable predictions about the stratum-2 stress phonology unexpectedly spotting transparent stratum-1 morphological relationships. In fact, stratal overlap facilitates a clear distinction between stratum-1 right-to-left (Latinate) stress assignment and stratum-2 left-to-right (essentially Germanic) stress assignment. Given the typical etymologies of the two strata, this makes sense.

The unexpected failure of strong stress preservation was interpreted in the preceding argument as the adoption of stratum-1 phonological behaviour by stratum-2 morphological forms. Conversely, if we factor out the secondary–primary stress contour and treat stress at this level as binary (as I demonstrated), then the unexpected occurrence of a weak stress 'preservation' effect discussed subsequently may be viewed as stratum-2 phonological behaviour displayed by stratum-1 morphological forms.

I make two further observations here, anticipating a return to the subject of modular overlap in the next chapter. Firstly, stratal overlap does not imply here that we have a defined set of morphological forms which simultaneously obey the model's stratum-1 and stratum-2 phonological predictions. Neither phenomenon is restricted to specific morphological processes. Rather, it is the (stress) phonology that straddles a divide which in morphological terms is quite unproblematic. And secondly, only the weak stress preservation effect can be formalised by invoking a failure of bracket erasure; strong stress preservation failure cannot. That means that bracket erasure is involved in but not solely responsible for safeguarding the integrity of modules such as stratum 1 and stratum 2 of the lexicon.

I will conclude my account of stratal overlap by discussing some further, unrelated examples suggesting stratal overlap, again showing both stratum-1 behaviour of stratum-2 forms and the converse.

4.5 More on stratal overlap

As I noted in section 4.2.3, stratum-1 forms have the phonotactic (and more generally, phonological) structure of morphologically simple items while on stratum 2, phonotactic configurations may occur in the vicinity of the internal morphological boundary which would be impossible in the absence of the boundary. Stratum 2 is simply morphological concatenation without phonological adjustment. Thus, the /dt/ and geminate /tt/ sequences in *bed-time* and *night-time*, the geminates in *soulless, keenness* as well as sequences such as the /tl/ in *weightless* and the /nl/ in *keenly* etc. are only possible in the presence of an internal boundary. While such clusters are relatively stable in diachronic terms (but see Götz 1971 and Faiß 1978 on diachronically 'obscured' compounds), geminates are known occasionally to simplify, as in *fully* and *wholly* (and probably more). This degemination could be accounted for by regarding these forms as stratum-1 products; but as in the case of *necessárily* etc. given in (3), there is no reason other than the phonology to treat such items as 'listed': their semantics is fully transparent. Once more, stratal overlap allows us to express phonological 'lexicalisation' in the traditional sense (Lipka 1994) without forcing us to make unwarranted claims on the semantic side.

A similar case is presented by base-final syllabic sonorants: as we saw in section 4.2.3, these are retained in stratum-2 suffixation (*metering, buttoning, summery*) but prevented on stratum 1 by the mechanisms of syllabification present there: *metrist, cylindric, baptismal* (Giegerich 1999: 263 ff.). However, a large number of apparently stratum-2 forms once again show stratum-1 phonological behaviour. Among these are some well-documented cases with concomitant semantic opacity (5a); but for others again no case for individual listing can be made on semantic grounds (5b):

(5) (a) twinkling ('short while')
         kindling ('chopped wood used to start a fire')
         lightning ('electric flash')
         coupling ('device connecting railway carriages')
         sprinkler ('device for watering gardens or extinguishing fires')

     (b) smuggler
         wrestler, wrestling
         fiddler
         settler

In contrast, less common forms such as *bottler* ('someone working in a bottling plant'), *haggler, wriggler* etc. are regularly trisyllabic. Adopting an earlier analysis by Chomsky and Halle (1968: 86), Mohanan (1986) takes the view that unlike its participle-forming counterpart, gerund-forming -*ing* (*twinkling, kindling* etc.) is attached on stratum 1; but that cannot be the reason for the non-syllabicity of such sonorants, as

we saw earlier. Semantic opacity rather than gerund status is the cause
of the stratum-1 provenance of such forms. So, the examples in (5a)
have semantic reasons for being listed, and hence for being stratum-1
constructions.

For (5b), again no such case can be made. The difference between bisyllabic *smuggler* and trisyllabic *bottler* is perhaps one of frequency, but not
one connected with semantic transparency. While Lipka (1994) does consider frequency to be a conditioning factor in lexicalisation (in the sense
of diachronic movement from stratum 2 to stratum 1), the stratum-1
analysis of *smuggler* on the grounds of its phonology alone, proposed
in Giegerich (1999: 34), is simplistic, assuming as it does that there is
a simple dichotomy between listed and rule-generated lexemes (see e.g.
Langacker 1987: ch. 1), which is expressed by the stratal distinction.

As I noted for other cases before, stratum-1–like phonological behaviour alone does not necessarily constitute a good case for the individual
listing of such forms. Rather, we are dealing once again with a stratum-2
form that is simply subject to the phonology of stratum 1. And note
again, in anticipation of a return to the topic in the next chapter, that
we are here not dealing with a specific morphological process, namely
-er suffixation, that misbehaves in this way. *Wrestling* is given in (5b) as
an example of a different process giving rise to sonorant non-syllabicity;
and in everyday speech there will undoubtedly be others. This is simply
a frequency-driven decay of phonological structure, which is not confined to specific morphological phenomena. Given that lexicalism, like
all formal grammar, has no direct encoding of frequency it has to posit
modular overlap.

The division of the set of English lexemes into a listed and a rule-
generated subset, as is implied by stratification models comprising
discrete strata, ignores the fact that the whole-word route and the decom-
position route in lexical accessing compete with each other. What is at
a premium is not memory space, as was assumed in much of the earlier
generative literature (before Halle 1973 perhaps), but processing time
(Baayen 1993; Frauenfelder and Schreuder 1992). A stratified lexicon, if
it is to model the accessing facts realistically, must take account of this
rather more complicated situation. The recognition that lexical strata can
overlap is the beginning of such a realistic modelling of the facts – even if
it does not exactly enhance the predictiveness of the formal model.

I conclude this chapter with a few observations regarding compounds
– not least in order to set the stage for the next chapter, which focuses on
compounds more sharply.

There is no dispute in the stratification literature that regular compounds are formed on stratum 2 – among those are synthetic compounds such as *watch-maker*, *train-spotting*, compounds with associative
modification (*mosquito net*, *baby oil*) and compounds with ascriptive

attribution such as *peanut oil, olive oil* – recall the preceding chapters especially on the distinction between the latter two categories, and its effects. All such constructions have it in common that they are endo-centric and right-headed. Not all have fore-stress; but the possible end-stress normally associated with phrasal constructions is also available to compounds.

There are, however, a number of compounds that are either exocentric or left-headed; and neither the exocentric (*bahuvrihi*) pattern – *redneck, shit-head, hatchback* – nor the left-headed pattern (*Princess Royal, court martial*) is productive. Such forms are either deliberately 'coined', or they are old loans from French. Certainly they are not formed by the compounding mechanisms found on stratum 2: they constitute listed and hence stratum-1 forms. But the problem with a stratum-1 analysis of such compounds is that they do not have the phonotactics associated with stratum 1: clusters occurring at boundaries, such as the /dn/ in *redneck*, the /th/ in *shit-head* etc., do not conform to the monomorphemic phonotactics of English that is obligatory in stratum-1 complex forms.

Rather tentatively, and aware that the lexical stratification model has a particular problem with the listing of complex forms (to be revisited in the next chapter), I suggest that such forms originate on stratum 1 but that they are subject to the phonotactics of stratum 2 – again a possible case of stratal overlap. This analysis is supported by the fact that such irregular compounds can enter into regular compounding but cannot have regular compounds as their constituents: *redneck fan, hatchback driver* are well-formed but *rearhatch-back, *lawcourt martial are impossible. This pattern is predicted by an analysis which treats *hatch-back* and *court martial* as stratum-1 forms, and regular compounds such as *rear-hatch* and *lawcourt* as stratum-2.

The lexicon–syntax divide, central to the expression of the Lexical Integrity Principle, which in turn played a major part in the original, 'strong' lexicalist hypothesis (Chomsky 1970), will be discussed in detail in the following chapter. But we have already seen that it is not unique in the grammar. It is paralleled by a very similar divide between the two strata of the English lexicon; and I have shown in this chapter that that divide is far from robust. Certain borderline phenomena can be accounted for only if the relevant modules are allowed to overlap.

Chapter 5

Lexical integrity?

5.1 On the nature of the lexicon–syntax divide

In the preceding chapter I looked in some detail at the purported 'divide' between stratum 1 and stratum 2 of the stratified lexicon I proposed for English in Giegerich (1999), drawing there on important early work by Kiparsky (1982), Selkirk (1982), Mohanan (1986) and others. I showed in Giegerich (1999: ch. 2) that a given process of morphological concatenation will typically apply on both sides of the stratal divide – that is, on both the root stratum and the word stratum. Moreover, we saw in Chapter 4 that the stratal divide itself is not as robust as had previously been asserted: for example, some characteristics of stratum 1 may still make their presence felt among certain forms which are otherwise of stratum-2 origin. Recall here forms such as *ordinárily* (also discussed by Burzio 1994), where a stratum-2 morphological structure combines with a stratum-1, stress-non-neutral prosodic pattern. The recognition of stratal overlap seems to account for the behaviour of such forms, albeit at the cost of considerably weakening the theory of base-driven stratification. It would have dealt a fatal blow to earlier, affix-driven models.

In this final chapter I turn to the other divide found in a lexicalist generative grammar of English: that between stratum 2 of the lexicon and the syntax. It may be argued that of the two divides now identified, this is in some way the more 'important' one (whatever may be meant by 'important' in this context). But that would be an illusion.

Of the three modules, the first two (stratum 1 and 2 of the lexicon) have in common that they concatenate sub-word units (or, in the case of compounds, word units) so as to produce members of lexical categories. They are distinct, as we saw, in that the first is essentially irregular and unproductive while the second is regular and productive. The second and third module (the lexicon's stratum 2 and the syntax) have in common that they are held to be regular in nature and fully productive. They are distinct in that the former produces members of lexical categories and the latter members of phrasal categories. Stratum 2 is therefore more closely related to stratum 1 than to the syntax in some respects, and more closely related to the syntax than to stratum 1 in others.

It was only under lexicalism that the divide between stratum 2 and the syntax acquired its perceived importance as the interface between the two traditional disciplines of morphology and syntax. For it was under lexicalism that a return to the traditional modularisation of the grammar was proposed, whereby the morphology and the syntax are held to be distinct not only regarding the nature and 'size' of the units which they concatenate, but also regarding the characteristics of the outcomes of such concatenation. Crucially, the morphology – in lexicalism integrated into the lexicon, whence the term – produces members of lexical categories ('words') while the outcomes of concatenations occurring in the syntax are members of phrasal categories.

The term 'lexicalism' refers to a stage in the evolution of generative grammar which began in the early 1970s and succeeded the period usually referred to as that of the '*Aspects* model' (after Chomsky 1965) or, if merely at the time, the 'standard model'. The *Aspects* model had recognised no fundamental distinction between the morphology – derivational or inflectional – and the syntax, instead placing importance on the divide we now refer to as the one between the lexical strata – in terms of Chomsky and Halle (1968: 86), the distinction between '+' and '#': the former are said to be 'internal to the lexicon' while the latter are assigned by syntactic transformations. In the *Aspects* model, the lexicon was an inactive repository of irregularity, while all concatenation would take place in the syntax. There was no separate morphology – a position not too dissimilar to more recent minimalist approaches and, like those, somewhat insensitive to the needs of the morphology.

Destruction would be derived from *destroy* by means of a transformation which differed merely in detail, not in principle, from the more familiar Passive transformation (as in *the men destroyed the house* → *the house was destroyed by the men*). Lees (1963) and Marchand (1969) pioneered the same approach for compounds, so that *sunrise, watch-maker* and such like would derive transformationally from underlying sentences such as *the sun rises, she or he makes watches*.

Moreover, allomorphy – such as that associated for example with the vowel shift alternation: *profane – profanity, wide – width, weep – wept –* was held to be non-distinct from the traditional phonology, and therefore an integral part of the grammar's phonological component as first formulated by Chomsky and Halle (1968). Therefore, morphology in the traditional sense had no separate, identifiable place in the *Aspects* model at all: its various roles in the grammar were allocated to the syntax and the phonology instead. It follows that the category Word had no systematic status in the grammar.

The lexicalist model was launched by Chomsky's 'Remarks on nominalization' (1970). There he presented an analysis, now considered classic, of the differences in behaviour between gerunds – (1b) below – and non-gerund nominalisations (1c), all of which would, under an *Aspects* account, have been derived from sentences such as those given in (1a). The summary I give here draws on Scalise (1984: 17 ff.) and Spencer (1991: 69 ff.).

(1)   (a)   Tom amused the children with his stories.
              Fred severely criticised the book.
              John doubted the proposal.

       (b)   Tom's amusing the children with his stories
              Fred's severely criticising the book
              John's doubting the proposal

       (c)   *Tom's amusement of the children with his stories
              Fred's severe criticism of the book
              John's doubt about the proposal

Gerunds inherit their sub-categorisation frames and other syntactic properties from their base verbs: those in (1b) are therefore transitive like *amuse, criticise, doubt*; and like verbs they are modified by adverbs. In contrast, nominalisations such as those in (1c) do not inherit the syntactic behaviour associated with their base verbs: they cannot take objects and are modified by adjectives rather than adverbs. Also, gerund formation is fully productive while for the formation of non-gerund nominalisations, a wide range of different morphological processes is available of which only a small sample (including conversion) is given in (1c). Nominalisations moreover tend to have a range of meanings well beyond the basic meaning 'act of', which invariably characterises gerunds: *retirement, marriage* and indeed *nominalisation* can denote both act and state, *construction* may be an act or an object, *revolution* has very little to do semantically with the base verb *revolve*.

Chomsky (1970) concluded that unlike gerunds, nominalisations such as those in (1c) cannot be derived transformationally without uncontrollable power being granted to transformations. And given, as we have seen, the wide range of semantic relationships available among the elements of compounds, the same is true for the transformational derivation of compounds from underlying sentences developed by Lees (1963) and Marchand (1969), and indeed for most of the derivational morphology in general. Instead, Chomsky (1970) called for a separate, 'lexical' derivation of morphologically complex words, governed by principles different from those of the syntax and subsequently to be explored in programmatic publications such as Halle (1973), Aronoff (1976) and others.

The reinstatement of the word level in the grammar thus promised to account for fundamental differences between syntactic and morphological constructions. Phrases and sentences are held to be fully transparent, and the mechanisms producing them are assumed to be fully productive. While sentences are uttered and then forgotten, words have a more permanent existence. Words are 'coined' and then often retained; and once retained in a speech community their meanings and often also their forms are prone to change through time, possibly losing the structural transparency they will initially have had. In the lexicalist model, the lexicon therefore has a dual function in that it is both a repository of words, which may or may not have internal structure, and an active component of the grammar (the 'morphology'), in which words are assembled from the familiar morphological building blocks by means of operations which may or may not be fully productive in the synchronic grammar. We shall see in this chapter that the latter function comes to it more easily than the former.

Lexicalism has led to the recognition of morphology as a self-contained sub-discipline of generative grammar, to the emergence of the lexicon as a separate, active component of the grammar, and eventually, with the development of lexical stratification and the theory of lexical phonology, to substantial progress in the understanding of the morphological, phonological and semantic structure of words. In its early form envisaged by Chomsky (1970), the theory did not, however, include a sub-theory of lexical stratification. No distinction was drawn there between the stratum-1 and stratum-2 morphologies; and the comparison of gerunds and the lexical nominalisations shown in (1) above is more informative about differences between the syntax and the stratum-1 morphology than it is about syntax–morphology differences in general, which can be rather less compelling when they involve stratum-2 derivation.

In exploring the lexicon–syntax divide, it is the differences between the syntax and the stratum-2 morphology that are of interest: some of the differences between the syntax and the morphology, noted by Chomsky (1970), may in reality be differences between the two lexical strata and hence no longer of relevance at this stage of the argument.

5.2 The purported integrity of the lexicon

5.2.1 *Lexical integrity and bracket erasure*

Recall from section 4.3 that under the bracketing conventions first proposed by Kiparsky (1982), prefixes are lexically stored as '[X', root as '[Y]' and suffixes as 'Z]'. Consider now the stratum-2 concatenation of the adjective A and the noun B (for example *green* and *house*) so as to form a compound noun, bracketed thus: $[[A]_{Adj} [B]_N]_N$ (where A and

B may contain further bracketing produced on stratum 2). Under the Bracket Erasure Convention, this structure enters the syntax simply as $[AB]_N$, so that for the purposes of the syntax, the phonological strings A and B are sub-strings of AB but no longer separate structural entities. No syntactic operation and no phonological operation drawing on syntactic structure (for example the phrasal stress rule) can 'see' the adjective and the noun embedded in the noun. On the other hand, the individual elements of a structure formed in the syntax, such as $[[A]_{Adj} [B]_N]_{NP}$, are available for syntactic operations. Thus, *an entirely green house, a red house and a green one* are well-formed. But these syntactic operations apparently cannot affect compounds: **an entirely green-house* and **a hen-house and a green one* are presumably ill-formed, as certainly are similar constructions involving, for example, synthetic compounds: **expensive watch-maker* (where the watches are expensive, not the craftsman), **a clock-maker and a watch one*. The literature calls this the Lexical Integrity Principle (Lapointe 1980; Di Sciullo and Williams 1987; Scalise and Guevara 2005), whereby syntactic processes can manipulate members of lexical categories ('words') but not their morphological elements. Note, incidentally, how the name seems to be a counter-example to what it denotes: *lexical* modifies *integrity*. (The similar 'No Phrase Constraint' proposed by Botha 1983, whereby syntactic phrases cannot be embedded in compound words, faces the same problem.)

Further questions regarding lexical integrity might be raised here; but they need no detailed discussion as they do not affect the argument. It is an unresolved issue for the theory, for example, whether all observed effects subsumed under the term 'Lexical Integrity Principle' are accounted for by the Bracket Erasure Convention. The overlap of lexical strata discussed in the last chapter suggests that bracket erasure – specifically its failure – may play a part in accounting for overlap phenomena, but it does not explain it all. So the maintenance of lexical integrity in turn may not be down to the Bracket Erasure Convention alone either. Ackema (1999: ch. 4) has argued that lexical integrity effects derive from other principles of syntactic architecture. It is also possible that the Lexical Integrity Principle has some kind of independent formal status in the grammar; in that case it remains unclear what its exact form actually is. But as we have seen, given the parallelisms between lexical integrity and stratal integrity, that last possibility now seems remote. We had no cause there to propose a stratal divide as a formal entity independent from the effects of the strata's separate characteristics and bracket erasure.

Whatever it is that causes such effects, independent principle or not, the notion of lexical integrity in some way defines the lexicon–syntax divide, expressing the traditional view whereby words are the atoms of syntactic structure. No syntactic operation can affect the elements of words.

In the coming sections I deal with a number of properties associated either with stratum 2 of the lexicon or with the syntax, following a line of reasoning begun in the present section as well as harking back to Chapter 1. These properties, syntactic, semantic and phonological, will serve as diagnostics for the lexical or syntactic provenance of a given complex nominal; I will assess the value of those individual diagnostics. And they will also, under the assumption of the validity of lexical integrity, enable certain predictions to be made regarding the simultaneous presence of such diagnostics in a given form. If, for example, fore-stress only occurs in the lexicon and the pro-form *one* only in the syntax (as in *a red house and a green one*), then a theory which features lexical integrity predicts that no fore-stressed form can allow pro-*one*. Much of this material is also addressed by Bauer (1998: 72 ff.); and see also Bisetto and Scalise (1999).

5.2.2 *Syntactic operations as diagnostics of phrasal status*

5.2.2.1 Co-ordination reduction

I begin with three phenomena which involve, or at least appear to involve, syntactic operations. The first is the phenomenon of co-ordination reduction, whereby in the co-ordination of two phrases containing an identical element, one instance of that element is deleted – the first of two identical heads and the second of two identical non-heads: hence *blue books and red books* → *blue and red books; red books and red pens* → *red books and pens*. The availability of this operation to *iron bars and steel bars* (→ *iron and steel bars*), *steel bars and steel weights* (→ *steel bars and weights*) would then seem to confirm the syntactic (that is, phrasal) nature of the forms involved (Bauer 1998: 74), unsurprisingly perhaps in that they also have end-stress.

However, co-ordination reduction is also found in fore-stressed forms which, for that stress reason and others, are clearly lexical:

(2)	(a)	wind- and water-mills	(b)	water courses and mills
		chemistry and physics teachers		physics teachers and students
		timber and pallet merchant		timber hauliers and merchants
		clock- and watch-maker		clock-makers and repairers

And to make matters worse (for lexicalists), co-ordination reduction can even affect prefixes and suffixes, as indeed in *pre- and suffixes* and in *weight- and shapeless*, thereby showing beyond doubt that co-ordination reduction has no respect for the lexicon's integrity.

This observation may then prompt us to salvage lexical integrity as a principle by asserting that co-ordination reduction is both a syntactic and a morphological operation, present therefore (in the form of two independent processes which happen to have identical effects) on both sides of the lexicon–syntax divide.

An analysis which differs in an interesting way from this *ad hoc* duplication of identical devices in the grammar has been offered by Booij (1985) and Wiese (1996b: 69 ff.), who argue that within complex words, the deletion of identical elements in co-ordination is not the same process as that found in the syntax but a phonological process, involving as it does the deletion of identical phonological material, minimally of the size of a single phonological word, provided that phonological material is repeated later in a structurally parallel position.

Thus, in German the elements of compounds freely delete, as do roots after prefixes and suffixes after roots, just as in English. But the process appears to be stylistically far more common in German than it is in English; and it is therefore significant that of the following German examples, the last is unequivocally ill-formed:

(3)   Tief- oder Hochebenen   ('low plains or high plains')
        be- und entladen   ('to load and unload')
        Ur- oder Ururoma   ('great- or great-great-grandmother')
        mütter- und väterlich   ('motherly and fatherly')
        *winz- oder riesig   ('tiny or huge')
                                  (Examples mostly from Wiese 1996b: 70)

In phonological theories which recognise the phonological word ('pword') as a unit of phonological constituency structure (for example Booij 1999; Hall 1999), morphological units which have pword status are roots, prefixes and consonant-initial suffixes but not vowel-initial suffixes. Therefore -*ig*, in the last example in (3), is the only element which fails to qualify for pword status. It is also the only element unable to delete: all other deleted elements, be they roots, prefixes of consonant-initial suffixes, are pwords and allow deletion.

A similar English example might be *thirst- and hungry*; but as noted above, the phenomenon is in any case stylistically rare in English when it involves elements of words, and its non-occurrence in a specific case therefore perhaps less significant.

So, co-ordination reduction among free forms in the lexicon differs from its syntactic counterpart (not analysed by Booij 1985 and Wiese 1996b) in that it is a phonological operation. If this alternative analysis of co-ordination reduction is accepted for English then not only do the examples in (2) pose no problem for lexical integrity, but the applicability of co-ordination reduction ceases to be a possible diagnostic for non-lexical status altogether.

5.2.2.2 Pro-*one*

The second possible diagnostic for phrasal status to be invoked here is the 'pro-*one*' operation – the replacement of the head of a noun phrase by the pro-form *one*, as in *a red book and a blue one*. There is no doubt that this is a credible syntactic operation (Hornstein and Lightfoot 1981; Stirling and Huddleston 2002) which, under the Lexical Integrity Principle, should therefore be able to distinguish between compounds and phrases in that it should be unable to affect the head of a compound. Indeed, to begin again with straightforward synthetic compounds, **a watch-maker and a clock one*, **a bird-watcher and a bat one* etc. are ill-formed. It is also, trivially, the case that pro-*one* only operates among word-sized units and not among prefixes and suffixes; hence **a singer and a write one* (= *writer*). The range of pro-*one* is not like that of co-ordination reduction, then: this seems to be a genuine operation of the syntax. But other cases are less straightforward.

Consider now the examples of ascriptive attribution, some of them *dvandvas* in the sense of Bauer (2008), listed in (4):

(4)   steel bridge
boy actor
rogue trader
luxury flat
actor-director
singer-songwriter

Pro-*one* is straightforwardly possible in most such cases – *a wooden bridge and a steel one, an adult actor and a boy one, a genuine trader and a rogue one, a basic flat and a luxury one*. Pro-*one* is unavailable in *olive oil* etc. for the independent reason whereby only count nouns are eligible. And if forms such as *a fulltime director and an actor one, a fulltime songwriter and a singer one* are odd then this may be connected with having an agent noun as an attribute. Perhaps *boy* and *rogue* are 'better' attributes than *actor* and *singer*.

If that is so, and if it is also true that pro-*one* is a reliable diagnostic of lexical integrity and phrasal non-integrity, then many ascriptive noun-plus-noun forms are phrasal, just like (more obviously perhaps) their adjective-plus-noun relatives; and like those they will be sporadically subject to lexicalisation and in the process possibly adopt fore-stress: *green-house, white-board, blackbird*, and with a noun modifier, *carrier-bag, man-servant, fighter-bomber*. Notably despite the stress difference, such forms too may have pro-*one*: *a long-distance bomber and a fighter one, a woman servant and a man one*. This is a problem for lexical integrity: as I noted before, the model predicts that fore-stressed forms cannot have pro-*one*; and if the end-stressed examples of nominal ascriptions are also lexical then they demonstrate the same problem.

The same probably goes for the examples of associative attribution by nouns listed in (5):

(5)   (a)   mountain railway   (b)   milk bottle
              school dinner   milk-weed
              village shop   milk-float
              summer fruit   milk-tooth
              university exam   flour mill
              garden path   windmill

There is likely to be some variation among speakers concerning the end-stressed, semantically fairly transparent examples in (5a); and some of those in (5b), with fore-stress, may also resist pro-*one*. But there does not appear to be a significant difference in pro-*one* behaviour between the two stress patterns. Pro-*one* resistance in individual cases seems, rather, to be driven by the semantics of associative modification.

Unlike in the case of ascriptive attribution, the entity denoted by the head noun can be associated with that denoted by the attribute in a variety of ways. A milk bottle is associated with milk in that it contains milk, while a milk-tooth has some other, more metaphorical association with milk. Thus it is possible to have *a water bottle and a milk one*, but probably not **a plastic bottle and a milk one*. Pro-*one* clearly requires a parallelism regarding the semantics of the attribution involved that is more finely grained than merely sharing the feature 'associative'. Hence **a shark tooth and a milk one* is probably unacceptable while *an adult tooth and a milk one* is fine. And it is possible to have *a windmill and a water one*, but **a windmill and a flour one* is less good – and this is not because *flour mill* is itself less amenable to pro-*one* (*a grain mill and a flour one* is again acceptable) but because wind and flour have different associations with mills, one powering them and the other produced by them. Bauer (1998) discusses more such cases of zeugma. And note that in the syntax, *a blue book and a good one* would also be odd: there is no reason to think this 'zeugma constraint' is specifically lexical.

A village shop is associated with a village in the sense that it is located in a village. Thus it is possible to have *an inner-city shop and a village one*; but in this case *a computer shop and a village one* may be better than the asterisked examples discussed in the preceding paragraph. If that is so, then the reason is probably that village shops are characterised not just by their locations but also, as noted before, by their merchandise. They sell certain goods – food and newspapers typically – and thus do have a semantic parallel with computer shops.

I turn finally to attribute–head constructions involving associative adjectives. As we saw in Chapter 2 above, pro-*one* applicability divides the set of such forms into two subsets – one lexical and one phrasal. It does so in an interesting way.

I distinguished three subsets of such constructions in Chapter 2: firstly, those where the relationship between noun and adjective is fairly straightforwardly 'associated with' – *tropical fish, bovine disease* etc., as in (6a) below; secondly, those where an argument–predicate relationship is present – *papal visit, presidential election* etc., such that the pope, for example, may be either the agent or the patient of the action of visiting ((6b) below); and thirdly, those whose interpretation requires significant, encyclopedic information, not provided in the adjective's lexical semantics: *musical critic, legal advisor* etc., at least to sustain the distinction between ascriptive and associative attribution in cases where both interpretations are available: (6c).

While all such forms in all other respects at least qualify for lexical status – recall for example that many of them have fore-stress – I showed in Chapter 2 that examples from the first subset will typically yield to pro-*one* while those of the other two subsets will not; and when they do then they will, significantly, often enforce an ascriptive, default interpretation where that interpretation is available. Here are some of the examples first discussed in section 2.5:

(6) (a) Is this the bovine strain of the disease or the feline one?
          Is he a rural policeman or an urban one?
          Is this a cold-water fish or a tropical one?

     (b) ?Do you mean the presidential murder or the papal one?
          ?Do you mean the parliamentary election or the presidential one?
          ?Do you need a back massage or a cardiac one?

     (c) *Is this the Home Office or the Foreign one?
          *Is he a constitutional lawyer or a criminal one?
          *Is he a theatrical critic or a musical one?
          *Is he an electrical engineer or an electronic one?
          *Is this a mental disorder or a nervous one?
          *Is he a financial advisor or a legal one?

For more detailed analysis, as well as for discussion of the data, the reader is referred back to Chapter 2 and to Giegerich (2005a). I note here merely that in these cases, pro-*one* appears to confirm a lexicon–syntax divide that was more speculatively drawn on semantic grounds above: cases where the full interpretation of the 'associated with' relationship involves argument structure, as in (6b), or where significant, ambiguity-avoiding encyclopedic information has to be present, as in (6c), rather than being able to be inferred, do not belong in the syntax but are lexical.

We see, then, that the pro-*one* operation produces somewhat surprising results when it is used as a test for the lexical or syntactic provenance of NN and AdjN forms. While we had hypothesised that such forms can be of either lexical or syntactic origin, compound or phrase, we have seen that the only constructions immune to pro-*one* are those involving argument–predicate relationships, clearly so in synthetic compounding and less clearly in associative AdjNs (**a clock-maker and a watch one*, **the presidential murder or the papal one* respectively).

The examples in (6c) show that under pro-*one*, associative adjectives default into ascription where such an interpretation is available; and it often is. As we saw in Chapter 2, this is to be expected. But in pro-*one* this adoption of an ascriptive sense again results in the zeugma problem, as in **a plastic bottle and a milk one*, discussed earlier. So the failure of (6c) to permit pro-*one* is again not syntactic but semantic, and tells us very little about lexical integrity. When the operation is seen to fail, in some instances of associative attribution, it does so not because the associative relationship as such does not permit pro-*one*, but because of differences in the precise nature of the attribution in the pro-*one* form and its antecedent: as we saw above, in associative attribution the applicability of pro-*one* is dependent on a rather finely grained parallelism in semantics of attribution, which not only has to be associative in both cases but moreover has to display similar kinds of association. Pro-*one* does not avoid associative attribution as such.

5.2.2.3 Phrases inside compounds

Under the assumption of lexical integrity, expressed perhaps by way of end-of-stratum bracket erasure (section 5.2.1 above), the elements of a word cannot be subject to syntactic operations. We saw in the preceding section that the pro-*one* operation does not fit well into that picture; now we consider the possibility that the elements of words may be amenable to modification. Note, firstly, that words embedded in prefixed words are not amenable: compare *not kind – unkind* and *not very kind – *unverykind*. Just as there was for pro-*one*, where *a singer and a writer* cannot give rise to **a singer and a write one*, there is a prima facie case to be made here for lexical integrity. Similar parallelism in synthetic compounds seems to strengthen that case: both pro-*one* and modification are ruled out: **a watch-maker and a clock one*, **expensive watch-maker* ('maker of expensive watches').

Once again the picture becomes more interesting in attributive NN forms. Is it possible for the individual nouns in such a compound to be pre-modified, thus forming noun phrases and resulting in compounds containing phrasal constituents? If it is not then modification (unlike pro-*one*, as we saw) provides us with a reliable diagnostic for compound status.

Lieber (1992) discussed slightly different forms, such as *Charles-and-Di syndrome*, *floor-of-a-birdcage taste*, *off-the-rack dress* etc. All of these must be noun compounds rather than phrases because, firstly, they may have the main stress on their first constituents (for example on *Di*); secondly, they do not conform with the pre-head modification patterns known for noun phrases; and thirdly, their second elements are not amenable to modification – **a floor-of-a-birdcage salty taste*. Assuming also that the first constituents of these compounds are genuine syntactic phrases, Lieber (1992: 14) concludes that '[r]ules of word formation must at least be allowed to refer to phrasal categories which are presumably generated as part of the syntax'.

However, the assumption whereby the first constituents in such constructions are generated in the syntax, rather than in the lexicon, is not uncontroversial. Bresnan and Mchombo (1995) and Wiese (1996a), for example, have argued that the embedded 'phrases' in *Charles-and-Di syndrome* etc. have the status of quotations, which may suggest some sort of lexical storage of such units – a position which is in turn disputed by Bauer et al. (2013: 488 ff.).

More in the mainstream of this discussion are compound-internal phrases, apparent or real, which result from attribution. One problem here is that, unlike pro-*one*, attribution resulting in AdjN and NN forms can itself be either lexical or syntactic; and while the difficulties of telling the two apart are well known (and indeed the main theme of this chapter), only syntactic attribution can be relevant here. We are therefore looking for noun phrases embedded in compound nouns.

This investigation should include cases of NNs embedded in NNs where the embedded NN is end-stressed, such as [[*garden shéd*] *manufacturer*], [[*model ráilway*] *enthusiast*] (recall (21) in Chapter 3): as we know, the embedded NNs here may be phrasal, given their end-stress. But given also that, as we saw in the preceding section, pro-*one* has to be expected to apply freely to such NNs regardless of their status, we are left without a means of ascertaining phrasal status and therefore side-step the discussion of these cases, from which little can be learned. I turn to AdjNs instead.

Some embedded AdjNs are given in (7) below, with ascriptive attribution in (7a) and associative attribution in (7b). As was discussed at length in Chapter 2, associative AdjN forms are beset by ambiguity regarding lexical or phrasal status, similar to end-stressed NNs; so we will avoid those as well. The following discussion will therefore focus on ascriptive examples such as *open door* etc. in (7a):

(7)	(a)	open door policy	(b)	solar panel installer
		cold weather payment		nuclear energy policy
		severe weather warning		atomic energy authority
		affordable housing policy		polar ice cap

ingrown toenail treatment
sexually transmitted disease clinic
flat roof specialist
solid fuel merchant

dental care insurance
lexical integrity principle
civil engineering degree

Most of the literature (for example Sproat 1985; Carstairs-McCarthy 2002: 82; 2005; Giegerich 2009a; but not Lieber 1992 and Bauer et al. 2013) seems to be in agreement that the phrases embedded in examples such as those in (6) are somehow lexicalised, perhaps displaying figurative or technical senses. Carstairs-McCarthy (2002: 82) contrasts in particular *open door policy* and *wooden door policy*, arguing that the former, a commonly used cliché, is fine while the latter is ungrammatical. I will disagree with part of this view in the next section.

It is striking that many, perhaps all, such embedded phrases are subject to jargon-specific technical definitions which they would not normally have when used in isolation. Thus, in *affordable housing policy, cold weather payment, severe weather warning*, the embedded phrases have technical definitions provided by the Social Security and Met Offices respectively: *affordable housing* in this context denotes housing with a specific maximum price per square metre, *cold weather* denotes an average of zero degrees Celsius or less over seven consecutive days; and to qualify for the term *severe weather*, thus triggering an official warning, weather must similarly meet a technically defined standard of badness.

Compare here the contrast in German between *starker Wind* ('strong wind', in everyday use) as opposed to *Starkwind* ('gale force 6 or 7 on the Beaufort Scale'). Similarly, *starker Regen* ('heavy rain') contrasts with *Starkregen* ('20 mm or more of rain in 6 hours or less'). German has stem-level compounding and relatively stable compound stress (Giegerich 1999; Wiese 1996b) and is able to express this contrast between naming and describing, such that typically the compound names a specific phenomenon and the phrase describes one (Schlücker and Hüning 2009). *Starkwindwarnung, Starkregenwarnung* ('gale/rain warning'), embedding *Starkwind* and *Starkregen* in compound nouns, are possible while *starker Wind, starker Regen* cannot be so embedded (**starke(r?) Windwarnung*).

In English, which has no stem-level compounding (because it has no stem level: Giegerich 1999: ch. 3) and no stable compound stress, the distinction is far less clear. Where the contrast is expressed, as for example in *bláck-bìrd* vs. *black bírd*, it tends to follow similar lines – species vs. described specimen; but where the contrast is not expressed, as for example in *severe weather* where there is no contrasting listed form **sevére-weather*, forms ambiguous in this way will tend to follow the everyday usage in isolation while under embedding they will have the technical sense forced on them.

Under such an analysis, forms such as *open door policy* and *cold weather payment* – and indeed *Lexical Integrity Principle* and *No Phrase Constraint*, apparent counterexamples to what they denote but also, like the others, subject to technical definition – are clearly compounds, in that particular theory generated on stratum 2 of the lexicon, but in the more theory-neutral and in fact stronger sense that they are compounds with an additional specific property – namely that of being lexically listed for their specific semantics even when they are formally regular. And if that is so and the forms in (7a) are lexically listed, then they cannot contain parts which are not lexically listed. This then motivates the 'cliché constraint' on phrases embedded in noun compounds such as those in (7a), and it enforces the technical definition of *severe weather* etc. under embedding but not in isolation. Phrase-like elements in lexically listed compounds must themselves be lexically listed. We will see below that in non-listed compounds this constraint does not hold.

An analysis reminiscent of this one was proposed by Spencer (1988) for apparent bracketing paradoxes such as *baroque flautist* ('someone who plays the baroque flute'), where the embedded form *baroque flute* is lexical, as opposed to **wooden flautist* ('someone who plays a wooden flute'), where *wooden flute* is phrasal. The former then undergoes suffixation with *-ist* while the latter, not being lexical, cannot. But Spencer's analysis does not solve the problem: *flautist* is an irregular, stratum-1 derivative of *flute* while lexical *baroque flute* is stratum-2, so this bracketing paradox persists within the lexicon; it merely affects the divide between stratum 1 and stratum 2 and not the one separating the latter from the syntax. *Wooden flautist* is merely a somewhat bigger problem if analysed as a bracketing paradox in that it involves stratum 1 and the syntax, across stratum 2.

A simpler analysis not involving insurmountable bracketing issues on the form side would be to treat *baroque* as an associative attribute ('flautist associated with the baroque period'). Note – and this is what is important here – that this analysis agrees with Spencer's inasmuch as it similarly correlates the grammaticality difference between *baroque flautist* and **wooden flautist* with lexical vs. syntactic provenance, in that associative attribution is lexical.

This now raises the question of whether the constraint on phrases inside compounds identified above also holds within compounds which are not lexically listed, taking us back from Spencer's *wooden flautist* to Carstairs-McCarthy's (2002) *wooden door policy*. I deal with this question in the following sections, after discussing the implications of this section's result for a lexicalist theory of formal morphology.

5.2.3 Listed semantics, regular form

Attempting to settle the question of how to distinguish compounds from phrases in English, Jespersen (1942: 137) claimed 'that we have a compound if the meaning of the whole cannot be logically deduced from the meaning of the elements separately'. While his claim does not strictly speaking imply that *all* compounds are of non-compositional semantics – he did not say *if and only if* – the context of the quotation clearly suggests that that was what he meant, curiously disregarding for example synthetic compounds, which typically are fully compositional (*watch-maker*, *coach-driver*), albeit different in their semantics from noun phrases in terms of their argument structure.

Nevertheless, Jespersen's flawed definition serves to highlight the fact that in compounds, perfectly regular form often goes with irregular, and hence listed, semantics, while noun phrases are expected to have compositional semantics. So, semantic irregularity may serve as a possible diagnostic for compound status, if not as a defining characteristic.

Some rather striking examples of semantic irregularity are found among phrasal names (see also Booij 2009), common for example in denoting bird species:

(8)   Yellow Wagtail
       Grey Wagtail
       White Wagtail
       Common Tern
       Arctic Tern
       Alpine Swift

Such species names give the impression of descriptive accuracy; but this impression is false in many cases. For example, while the Yellow Wagtail is striking for its partly yellow colour, the Grey Wagtail is almost as yellow and the White Wagtail is only partially, and not strikingly, white. In Britain, not an Arctic country, the Arctic Tern is more common than the species called Common Tern; and the Alpine Swift is not the only Swift to occur in the Alps and also occurs in many Mediterranean countries. Clearly, the ascriptive adjectives which figure in such names are semantically unreliable. These are simply names agreed by the ornithological community, and hence listed despite their formal regularity. While the head nouns serve a classificatory purpose in denoting family membership, the adjectives are at best of some mnemonic or perhaps contrasting value but essentially arbitrary.

Unsurprisingly, the elements of phrasal names such as these are unavailable for individual modification: *an extremely Common Tern, *a totally White Wagtail. If such modification were to occur then only a phrasal interpretation of the whole form would be possible. This aspect of lexical integrity follows from both the listed nature and the name status of the construction. Listed forms cannot contain unlisted material. Therefore, to change *White Wagtail* to *Totally White Wagtail* is simply to add *Totally* to what is listed and thereby to add a different name to the list of names for bird species. It so happens that there is no species of that name; but that clearly is not a linguistic problem.

It may be argued here that phrasal names are an unusual type of lexical construction, and that specific kinds of semantic behaviour are to be expected of names (Anderson 2004). This is true, but while irregular, listed semantics does not serve to define compound status, as we saw, it must nevertheless be expected to occur in compounds. Phrasal names are not unusual in that respect.

There are other cases of non-compositional ascriptive attribution, for that reason also presumably lexical on a par with phrasal names. In (9) below I give some similar examples (mostly from Bauer 2004) which do not involve species names but display the same semantic weakness on the part of the ascriptive attribute, such that for example black tea is not literally black, white coffee not really white, and noise is incapable of having a colour at all. Consequently there can be no *dazzlingly white noise* or *coffee*.

(9)   black tea
       brown rice
       white grapes
       white noise
       white coffee
       white meat

But while in ascriptive attribution, semantic unpredictability appears to be sporadic, identifiable only on a case-by-case basis, in associative attribution its presence is systematic. The reason is that associative attribution is by definition semantically underspecified, such that the entity denoted by the head is in some way 'associated with' the entity denoted by the attribute, but the nature of the association is not expressed by the linguistic form.

(10)   mountain railway
       school dinner
       village shop
       summer fruit
       university exam
       garden path
       morning coffee
       country house

The examples given in (10), familiar from earlier discussion, are fairly transparent in that the nature of the head–attribute association can be largely or even completely inferred. Mountains are places; hence a mountain railway is associated with mountains in that it is an object *located among* mountains. Summer is a season; hence summer fruit is fruit associated with that particular season in that it grows in that season. And so forth.

Note, however, as already discussed earlier, that *village shop* has an association with a village not only in that it is in that place but also in that it conveniently serves the village with the particular kind of merchandise called for at short notice. Similarly, a country house is not just any house located in the country but one that is also likely to have certain architectural characteristics, given the historical origin of the term *country house*. On closer inspection most compounds containing associative attribution will show traces, however small, of non-compositional semantics. Here, in instances of which some are already familiar, are some more extreme cases of meanings which have to be listed:

(11) milk bottle   'bottle for containing milk'
      milkman   'man who delivers milk'
      milkmaid   'woman who milks cows or works in a dairy' Molkerei
      milk-float   'vehicle which delivers milk'
      milk-fever   'disease caused by lack of the calcium contained in milk'
      milk-tooth   'tooth present while young mammal is still drinking milk'
      milk-weed   'weed with sap like milk'
      milk-wort   'plant formerly supposed to encourage lactation in cows'
      milk-tart   'tart made with milk'
      milk-leg   'swelling of legs after childbirth'
      milk-round   'fixed route on which milk is delivered'

Notably, compounds such as these are completely regular in formal terms: they are simple noun-plus-noun combinations, with the head on the right, in line with the rest of the regular morphology (Williams 1981) and an associative attribute on the left. It is the essentially underspecified nature of associative attribution which ensures that for every such form, a wide range of possible senses is available, which are therefore not predictable from the form, and of which arbitrarily one is selected and listed. Listed 7 semantics therefore has to be expected in all cases of associative attribution even where some elements of the semantic relationship (as in *country house*, *village shop*), or perhaps most elements (*mountain railway*, *morning coffee*), can be inferred: the semantics listed for a given form is not necessarily redundancy-free. This is why compounding is so versatile.

A number of attempts have been made to further sub-categorise the two types of attribution, ascriptive and associative, ranging from the comparatively simple classifications of semantic relations proposed by for example Levi (1978) and Fanselow (1981) (see Olsen 2000 on the latter), to descriptively detailed lists of possible compound meanings in Marchand (1969) and Adams (1973, 2001). But the view I take here is that these more detailed sub-categories of semantic relations internal to attribute–head constructions are wholly or partly determined by the lexical semantics of the attribute and the head, and hence not really 'basic' in the sense of being maximally free of redundancy. What is basic in this respect is the distinction between ascriptive and associative attribution: if this distinction were similarly predictable from the semantics of the participants then doublets such as *toy factory* (ascriptive: 'factory which is a toy', associative: 'factory for toys') and similarly *steel warehouse, driving instructor* etc. (previously discussed in Chapters 2 and 3) could not occur.

In a stratified lexicon, this property of being listed, for either irregular form or irregular meaning, is a defining characteristic of stratum-1 forms, as we saw in Chapter 4; but stratum-2 forms are assumed to be generated by productive rules and assumed to be both formally and semantically regular. There is no provision for the semantic underspecification which characterises productive nominal compounding using associative attribution. (For discussion, albeit in different terms, see Allen 1978, 1980; Kiparsky 1982.) It would appear that compounding is unique among stratum-2 processes in this respect; but it is a feature which causes problems for any form-based derivational theory of word structure. It does so in at least two respects. The first problem is that such theories are based on the well-known generativist assumption of a strict dichotomy of derivation-by-rule vs. listing, where the former is assumed to be of limitless capacity while the memory space needed for the latter is at a premium (Pinker 1999). We now know that this is not the case: what is at a premium in producing or perceiving speech is processing time, not memory space, and therefore there is no simple dichotomy but a competition between the two, where listing occurs not merely, necessarily, due to irregularity but also driven by frequency: high token frequency causes complex forms to embed in the memory, facilitating fast retrieval; low token frequency inhibits fast retrieval from memory, giving derivation by rule the competitive advantage (Frauenfelder and Schreuder 1992; Baayen 1993).

In defence of the formal theory one would then have to argue that the existence of a separate repository of listed items as a source of regular complex forms, alternative to assembly of such forms in real time, is a mere processing issue, which has no bearing on the nature of the formal grammar itself. But that recognition weakens any claim that the grammar models the procurement of morphologically complex lexical material in a 'psychologically real' way.

Another problem with that position is this. If the possible listing on semantic grounds of formally regular items is a mere processing matter for the speaker, rather than being incorporated into the grammar as a formally expressed alternative to a derivation, then such listing cannot have any impact on the formal characteristics of such items. And it seems as though some of the characteristics of phrasal names discussed earlier, as well as further features to be identified below, might falsify this claim. In the following section I will therefore discuss compound nouns known not to be listed.

5.2.4 Unlisted semantics: anaphoric compounding

I noted in section 5.2.2.3 that Carstairs-McCarthy (2002) regards *wooden door policy* as ungrammatical in contrast to *open door policy*, arguing that the embedded phrase in the latter is of a cliché-like nature and that only phrases of that kind, lexicalised in some way, can be contained in compounds. This also seems to confirm the Lexical Integrity Principle, such that lexical forms can only contain material which is itself lexical.

In section 5.2.3 I discussed the issue of clichés and more generally that of listed semantics further, hypothesising that listed compounds are able to contain phrasal material as long as that material is itself listed. My hypothesis thus differs from Carstairs-McCarthy's in seeing the cause of any constraint relevant here in the nature of the embedding compound, rather than in the nature of the embedded phrase. *Open door policy* conforms to Carstairs-McCarthy's hypothesis because of the clichéd nature of *open door*; and it does to mine on the reasonable assumption that it is a listed compound (recall section 5.2.3). *Wooden door policy*, where *wooden door* is a phrase which has no obvious reason for being listed or lexicalised, is ruled out absolutely (and explicitly) by Carstairs-McCarthy's hypothesis, while mine predicts its grammaticality as long as the embedding compound is *not* listed.

I believe Carstairs-McCarthy's grammaticality judgement on *wooden door policy*, and more generally his hypothesis, to be incorrect: contexts which allow such forms can in fact be found. The following two anecdotes will serve to set the stage for a more general discussion.

Firstly, an imaginary building contractor might state that 'it is our policy not to fit wooden doors in premises licensed for the storage of flammable materials. This *wooden door policy* ensures compliance with . . .'. Note that the compound is interpretable in this context only because its semantics has been spelled out in the preceding sentence.

Secondly: a similar context arose in my department some years ago when a visiting lecturer was scheduled to give two talks, of which one was on ethnological conditioning in phonological change. A last-minute email message informed us that 'John's talk on X will go ahead today but his *ethnological conditioning lecture* has been postponed till tomorrow 2 p.m.'.

The two anecdotes, one fictitious and one real, have in common that in both cases the compound containing an unlisted phrase is a nonce formation, whose interpretability depends crucially on information which has been given previously in the same discourse. *Wooden door policy* denotes a policy associated with wooden doors, where 'associated with' means specifically 'governing the positions in which they may be fitted' and not for example the colour in which they are painted. An *ethnological conditioning lecture* is a lecture associated with the ethnological conditioning of something, specifically one *about* the ethnological conditioning *of sound change*. Without such context, the compound would be impossible, as in **tomorrow John will give an ethnological conditioning lecture*.

So, it seems possible for English compounds to breach lexical integrity in the sense of phrase-inside-compound if they are nonce formations, provided that information about the precise nature of the semantic association of the head with the embedded phrase is given by the preceding context, to which the compound anaphorically refers. Without such anaphoric link, compounds of that kind would be near-incapable of interpretation. (See Downing 1977, as well as ten Hacken 2013 on 'deictic compounds'.) Note, incidentally, that it is not possible to explain compounds containing phrases away by calling them phrases overall: both our examples must be compounds on the evidence of their fore-stress (while the embedded phrases unsurprisingly have end-stress).

A very similar but in many ways more interesting case is presented by compounds in headlines – 'Headlinese' compounds for short (Mårdh 1980). Price (2014) investigated a specific subset of such headlines, namely those found on the BBC Scotland News front page (http://www.bbc.co.uk/news/scotland) as links to news stories on other pages; similar examples can be found as headlines above articles, and on newspaper billboards.

Price collected some 150 examples between May and November 2013; I give a sample in (12) below and another in (13), in each case with a date recorded by Price and my bracketing and gloss.

(12)   (a)   [[[*Bridge toll*] *rise*] *inquiry*] *to start*
               'inquiry into a rise in bridge tolls' (27/5/2013)
         (b)   [[*Badger* [*pilot cull*]] *start*] *sparks anger*
               'start of an experimental cull of badgers' (1/6/2013)
         (c)   [[[*Phone row*] *murder*] *boy*] *guilty*
               'boy accused of a murder prompted by a row over a mobile phone'
               (4/6/2013)
         (d)   [[*Prisoner* [*vote right*]] *bid*] *thrown out by MPs*
               'proposal to give voting rights to prison inmates' (6/6/2013)

(e) [[*Tram system*] [*cable work*]] *to begin*
     'cable-laying work for the tram system' (11/6/2013)
(f) [[*Child* [*heart surgery*]] *report*] *due*
     'report on heart surgery for children' (12/6/2013)
(g) [[[*Pot hole*] *damage*] *compensation*] *doubles*
     'compensation for damage caused by pot holes' (15/6/2013)
(h) [[[*Hill murder*] *appeal*] *car*] *on Crimewatch*
     'car shown in an appeal for information about a murder on a hill'
     (21/6/2013)
(i) [[*Boat wreckage*] *fisherman*] *rescued*
     'fisherman searched for after the wreckage of a boat was found'
     (2/7/2013)
(j) [[[*Edinburgh flat*] *murder*] *man*] *convicted*
     'man charged with a murder committed in a flat in Edinburgh'
     (8/7/2013)

For the interpretations of highly complex compounds like this, the grammar offers only the feature of right-headedness, and the two options of associativeness and ascriptiveness to facilitate a semantic interpretation of the head–modifier relationship. Neither the choice between these options nor the bracketing can be inferred by the reader of these headlines, although in the spoken version (if there were one) the stress contour might give some help towards both. The glosses provided above (and in (13) below) are therefore highly dependent on the reader's pre-existing knowledge of the news item which they refer to. In most cases they could not have been provided without knowledge of that background story.

The examples show the truly impressive range of interpretations available to associative attribution. In some of these examples, semantic interpretation is reasonably straightforward by inferring the nature of the head–modifier association – for example in (12a.e.g). But in other examples the bracketing and the interpretation of the head–modifier association depend on their contexts in the news discourse – for example (12b.c.i). These cases refer to, for example, a proposed experimental ('pilot') cull of badgers (12b) rather than some cull of badger pilots. Similarly the murder case referred to in (12c) had previously been reported, as had the discovery of a wrecked fishing boat (12i).

It would appear, then, that Headlinese compounds may be used to test the hypothesis whereby unlisted compounds allow the embedding of phrases. Headlinese compounds are not listed. They are nonce formations, whose semantic interpretation depends entirely on their context. This, then, is linguistic compounding in its purest form – compounding without listing.

Price (2014) has a number of examples which contain adjectival modification:

(13) (a) *Irish plan [[plain [cigarette pack]] law]*
'law making plain packaging for cigarettes obligatory' (29/5/2013)

  (b) *[[[Sexual assault] [CCTV image]] man] traced*
'man shown in CCTV footage of a sexual assault' (30/5/2013)

  (c) *[[New [city school]] plans] unveiled*
'plans for a new school in the city' (30/5/2013)

  (d) *[[[[Missing teen] murder] suspect] arrest]*
'arrest of a suspect in connection with the murder of a missing teenager' (30/5/2013)

  (e) *[[[[Snow-hit farmers] aid] plea] success]*
'success of a plea for aid made by farmers who have been affected by snow' (4/6/2013)

  (f) *[[Fife [violent crime]] rise] causes concern*
'rise of violent crimes committed in Fife' (9/6/2103)

  (g) *[[[Toxic chemical] leak] firm] fined*
'company guilty of causing the leak of toxic chemicals' (21/6/2013)

  (h) *[[Live [[child abuse] images]] warning] issued*
'warning of live images showing child abuse' (1/7/2013)

  (i) *[[Alleged [European [horsemeat]]] trader] re-emerges*
'trader of what was alleged to be European horse-meat' (3/11/2013)

  (j) *[[[[Gay clergy] book] row] priest] removed*
'priest implicated in a row about a book which names gay clergy' (18/11/13)

It may well be the case that the AdjN forms contained in some of these examples are lexicalised like Carstairs-McCarthy's (2002) example of *open door*, discussed earlier. *Sexual assault, violent crime, toxic chemical* (13b.f.g) may be in that category and hence of little interest here; there is no dispute that unlisted compounds may embed listed material. What is of interest here is the embedding of unlisted material. And there are indeed examples of such forms which are very clearly phrasal, on a par with Carstairs-McCarthy's *open door*: *plain cigarette pack* (13a), *new city school* (13c), *missing teen* (13d), *alleged European horsemeat* (13i), *gay clergy* (13j) and possibly others. In some of these cases the bracketing, crucial to semantic interpretation, could only be ascertained through knowledge of the news item, notably in (13c.i.j). But once the structure is established no problems regarding the modifier–head semantics arise in such cases of embedded phrases with ascriptive attribution, unlike in the associative attribution found in (12).

The remarkable depth of embedding which is possible in Headlinese compounds is clearly register-specific – we would be unlikely to say, *That man over there is the gay clergy book row priest*. But it is probably not for register reasons that indefiniteness seems even less likely to be available to these compounds (just as it is to *ethnological conditioning lecture*)

– even with the shorter specimens. *He is a gay clergy book row priest* may be unlikely due to its sheer length, but *he is a boat wreckage fisherman* must be ruled out for other reasons – contrast *he is a boat-wreckage survivor*, with the same bracketing and more readily inferable semantics.

Unavailability of indefiniteness may perhaps have several unrelated causes, which may come together in the impossibility of context-free interpretation: the Headlinese compounds discussed here can have an anaphoric function only, not a naming function and not even one of properly describing. But, as the identical behaviour of my initial non-Headlinese examples of *wooden door policy* etc. shows, it would be wrong simply to disregard Headlinese compounds in this analysis on the possible grounds of their 'not being real English'. They may have marginal register-specific features but they are not structurally different.

I conclude, then, that nonce formations in anaphoric and/or Headlinese contexts support the hypothesis whereby it is not compounds in general but, specifically, listed compounds which disallow the embedding of phrases. Not for the first time, lexicalism clearly has a problem here in that the examples discussed in this section violate the Lexical Integrity Principle. But these violations, themselves a serious matter, are merely a symptom of a deeper problem in the theory – indeed, as I noted above, of any form-based derivational theory: its difficulty in expressing listed outputs of formally regular and fully productive processes. Ironically, lexicalism does not seem able to give us a theory of lexicalisation (Hohenhaus 2005; Brinton and Traugott 2005; ten Hacken and Thomas 2013; Thomas 2013).

5.3 Compounds in no-man's land

5.3.1 Lexical non-integrity

There can be no doubt that under a lexicalist modularisation of the grammar, compounding is a lexical phenomenon: compound nouns, for example, are members of the lexical category Noun; and it is only the lexicon's remit to produce members of lexical categories. Specifically in a stratified lexicon compounding is situated on the final stratum: not only is it fully productive and regular on the form side; it also interacts fairly freely with processes of the derivational morphology which are for independent reasons known to be on stratum 2: *rule-governedness, to re-aircondition, to wall-paper, to grandstand* etc. (Kiparsky 1982).

This uncontroversial analysis receives support from the phonology – the fore-stress found in many compounds is confined to the lexicon. It occurs in the syntax only under specific conditions determined by its pragmatic and semantic context, and is there never lexically conditioned. And the semantics, too, backs a lexical analysis: as we have seen, many compounds are formally regular but semantically non-compositional, a phenomenon found in the lexicon but not in the syntax (though it is not expected on stratum 2 of the lexicon either).

The lexicalist model predicts for compounds, then, that they should be subject to lexical integrity: syntactic processes are predicted to be able to manipulate the whole compound but not its elements: the syntax should not be able to 'see' its internal structure any more than it can identify, and interact with, other kinds of morphological complexity. The Lexical Integrity Principle, whatever its precise status and formulation (recall section 5.2.1), is a cornerstone of lexicalist theorising.

In section 5.2 I studied a number of syntactic operations which freely apply to the constituents of noun phrases and which, under lexical integrity, should never be able to affect the components of compounds.

Thus, in section 5.2.2.2 I discussed the pro-*one* operation as a possible diagnostic for lexical status. I showed that true immunity to pro-*one* is found among NNs only where those are synthetic compounds (**a clock-maker and a watch one*). It is also found among AdjNs, possibly, where the adjective is associative and in an argument–predicate relationship with its head – a feature those AdjNs share with synthetic compounds: **the presidential murder and the papal one*.

I then found, surprisingly, that all other AdjN and NN compounds make their elements available to pro-*one* in principle, regardless of their stress and regardless of the nature of their attribution, associative or ascriptive. Failure to apply in **a windmill and a flour one*, for example, is due to the non-parallelism – I called it zeugma – of the associative relationship in *windmill* and *flour mill* (Bauer 1998). The awkwardness of *a constitutional lawyer or a criminal one*, where *criminal* favours an ascriptive interpretation, will have similar reasons. So, while perhaps more tightly constrained on the semantic side than has been recognised (Stirling and Huddleston 2002), pro-*one* is in principle available to the elements of compounds, with the only real exception being those which display argument–predicate relationships: synthetic compounds and certain associative AdjNs. Such relationships are clearly lexical and probably lack a counterpart in the noun phrase.

In subsequent sections I looked at the occurrence of noun phrases in the non-head positions of nominal compounds: *ethnological conditioning lecture* etc. In configurational terms, this would be a structure produced in the lexicon which contains material produced by the syntax – an impossibility under lexicalist assumptions, given that in derivational terms, modification (such as that by *ethnological*) is another syntactic operation to which the individual elements of compounds are predicted by lexical integrity to be immune.

I argued that any constraints on the modification of the elements of compounds are due not to the compound status of the construction but to the additional feature of being a compound which is *listed*. The naming function typically performed by nouns makes them prone to listing even if they are compounds which have the internal structure of phrases. Thus, *White Wagtail* is a phrasal name for a bird species. *Totally White Wagtail* is possible only where *White Wagtail* is interpreted as a phrase rather than a listed phrasal name, or perhaps to denote a different, hypothetical species.

Compounds which are nonce formations without a naming function, and which for that reason and others are not listed, have no constraint banning embedded phrases: for example forms with anaphoric functions (*John's ethnological conditioning lecture*) or headlines referring to news items (*Gay clergy book row priest*). The constraint perceived by Carstairs-McCarthy (2002) whereby compounds can contain phrases only where those are clichés or names (*open door policy*, *severe weather warning*) is in reality a constraint on *listed* compounds: it bans unlisted material from occurring within listed forms. It is not a constraint on compounds as such, although it does hold in synthetic compounds. *Expensive watch-maker* cannot in any context denote a maker of expensive watches.

So, there are two syntactic operations which potentially affect the elements of NN compounds but should be barred from doing so by lexical integrity: pro-*one* and modification. (Recall that a third operation, co-ordination reduction, was argued to be phonological in nature and hence irrelevant here.) The preceding sections have shown beyond doubt that this prediction, central to lexicalist theory, is met in the case of affixation, trivially, and in the case of synthetic compounding. But compounds involving attribution, both ascriptive and associative, are not in principle subject to lexical integrity. When they appear to be, then this is in reality due to different reasons, some of which, such as the avoidance of zeugma, may also hold in the syntax.

5.3.2 Overlapping modules

Some of the findings of this chapter – for example that fore-stressed NNs or AdjNs should be able to undergo pro-*one* or attract modifiers to their individual constituents – are calamitous for lexicalists whose theory posits a strict lexicon–syntax divide which enforces lexical integrity. On the other hand, given what we found out in Chapter 4 about the divide between the strata of the lexicon, and specifically about that divide's lack of robustness, such findings should not surprise us. In this final section I shall therefore sketch a model of the lexicon–syntax interface which is consistent with the behaviour of English NNs and AdjNs. I do not claim that this model will hold for other languages, nor that it is comprehensive for this or any other such interface phenomenon found in English.

Let us first deal with, and see off, synthetic compounds (*watch-maker* etc.): the integration of such forms into a strict lexicalist model presents no problems. They invariably have fore-stress: I showed in section 3.3.2 that Bauer et al.'s (2013: 447) alleged counterexample of *party léader* forms part of a well-defined set and that it can therefore be accounted for. These compounds also do not allow syntactic operations to affect their elements. And given that they express an argument structure which does not occur in the syntax – subsective modification, discussed in Chapter 1, is their nearest syntactic equivalent but lacks the argument structure – we have no difficulty in regarding synthetic compounding as truly lexical. This is a stratum-2 process, fully productive and semantically transparent as is expected of processes on that stratum. One might ask here whether the inability of pro-*one* to affect the heads of synthetic compounds is due to their lexical status or their argument structure. I tentatively suggest the latter. This does not affect the diagnosis of synthetic compounds as lexical (there are other arguments for that position, as we have seen) but it also covers the *papal murder* cases, which in other respects (for example because of their end-stress) share the behaviour of the class to be discussed next.

The attribute–head form – a form which, unlike synthetic compounding, is found in both compounds and phrases – shows an unruly mix of behaviour associated with the syntax and behaviour expected in the lexicon. In particular, the phenomena whose possible co-occurrence needs to be modelled are the following.

Firstly, English NNs and AdjNs may have fore-stress or end-stress.

Secondly, both fore-stressed and end-stressed forms freely allow both pro-*one* and modification for their constituents. Constraints on internal modification hold only among listed forms.

Thirdly, both fore-stressed and end-stressed forms may be semantically non-compositional.

As a first attempt let us hypothesise that the availability of a compound's element to syntactic operations is due to a failure of the Bracket Erasure Convention in the transition from the lexicon to the syntax, so that the internal bracketing of such compounds, although for independent reasons produced in the lexicon, is visible to the syntactic operations in question. Bracket Erasure failure played a part in the stratal overlap discussed in Chapter 4. But this would result in an implausible derivational path for some complex compounds, such that those in (13) above, containing phrases, are first constructed without the phrasal modifiers, and that those are later added into the existing structure. *Gay clergy book row priest* (13j), for example, would be generated in the lexicon as *clergy book row priest*, and *gay* attached to *clergy* (not to *priest* – recall that this is a book about gay clergy) after the form has entered the syntax. Similarly, *Fife violent crime rise* (13f) would presumably emerge from the lexicon as *Fife crime rise*, to have *violent* inserted by the syntax. This derivational path is implausible, and in any case not needed for the compounds in (12), which seem to have no problem being constructed lexically bottom-up but show no other differences in behaviour which might result from this fundamental derivational difference. Moreover, Bracket Erasure failure does not account for the other aspects of uncertain or mixed behaviour enumerated above. In which module is, for example, *Fife* attached to *crime rise*? While we are clearly on the right track with an analysis whereby the elements of such compounds are visible to the syntax, Bracket Erasure failure alone is not the right way to express this.

Instead I propose a more radical analysis. I leave aside unequivocally phrasal instances of ascriptive adjectival attribution such as *green house*, *black bird* etc. These clearly belong in the syntax, where their attributes can be freely manipulated as in *so green a house, the blackest bird* etc., as Sweet (1900: 25) was probably the first to point out. These are as unproblematic as syntactic structures as synthetic compounds are as lexical structures. But there is a grey area between the two extremes.

For those attribute–head forms relevant here I suggest that they are generated in an 'area' of the modularised derivation which is simultaneously part both of (stratum 2 of) the lexicon and of the syntax, an area therefore where the two modules overlap with each other like slates on a roof. Let us say this overlap is the site where nominal attributes are attached and where associative attribution takes place. Ascriptive adjectival attribution of the *green house* kind takes place later in the derivation, in the syntax. This ordering ensures that associative and noun attributes are always nearer their heads than ascriptive adjectives are, expressing the ordering constraint established in Chapter 2.

The overlap area of the two modules is part of the lexicon firstly in the sense that it produces complex lexical nominals, secondly in that it makes fore-stress (assigned by a rule in the stratum-2 phonology) available to its outputs, and thirdly in that it produces (in associative attribution) outputs which are amenable to listing on semantic grounds. *uncompositional*

The overlap area is part of the syntax in that, firstly, it produces phrase-like complex nominals. Secondly, it allows syntactic operation such as pro-*one* and pre-modification to interact relatively freely with compounding, effectively admitting phrases into compounds but subject to independent and more general structural constraints whereby, for example, no noun phrase can be the head of a compound noun: only left sisters are available to pre-modification. Thirdly, the overlap expresses the availability of end-stress (assigned by a postlexical rule referring to syntactic constituency) to compound nouns, thereby expressing the insight that forms such as *village shop* have the stress pattern of phrases, and not just some exceptional, non-fore-stress pattern (although end-stress is of course the only alternative to fore-stress). So the overlap simply makes the lexical and phrasal stress patterns available to forms generated there. It makes no predictions as to which form will adopt which pattern. I believe this lack of prediction to be exactly the right outcome, and not merely because making no predictions is better than making wrong predictions.

Work on the phonology of English compounds in recent years has identified tendencies rather than robust generalisations. For example, I argued in Giegerich (2009a) and Chapter 3 above that, phrase-like, relative transparency favours end-stress: *stone wall, summer fruit* etc. But some transparent NNs have fore-stress, as for example many or all of the list of culinary oils given in (16a) of Chapter 3. I also argued that associative attribution favours fore-stress while – again, phrase-like – ascription does not; hence fore-stress in forms such as *dental hospital, legal advice* as well as in the non-culinary oils in (16b) of Chapter 3. But again, *musical critic, electrical engineer* have end-stress, as do *country house* and *village shop*. Moreover, a number of larger-scale empirical investigations into the distribution of these stress patterns have had probabilistic outcomes. In particular, work by Ingo Plag and his collaborators, cited in Chapter 3 above and summarised in more detail by Bauer et al. (2013: section 19.3.3), has shown that such distributions are driven by a variety of possible factors and that they strongly resist categorical results. The firm patterns that do arise, for example in association/ascription doublets such as *tóy factory* vs. *toy fáctory*, are blocking effects, in which the associative form is listed with the fore-stress favoured by associative attribution and thereby enforces the ascriptive sense in the freely generated end-stressed form (section 3.3.5 and Giegerich 2001).

Note that under this account, the compound–phrase distinction is predicted to be effectively neutralised for the kind of construction discussed here. This neutralisation seems to be entirely unproblematic in terms of the structure and syntactic distribution of such forms (Bauer 1998: 83 ff.); but in formal grammar, which places a high value on category distinctions (Rauh 2010: chs 4 f.), a model which produces lexical and phrasal categories in distinct modules can express such neutralisation only through overlap. At any rate, if there were a real distinction to be drawn between words and phrases within this set of forms then somebody would probably have found out how to draw it by now. The debate has, after all, been going on for more than a hundred years (Sweet 1900; Bloomfield 1933; Koziol 1937 . . .) without being resolved.

Various kinds of evidence have accrued in this chapter which suggest that listing has a role to play in explaining the behaviour of certain compounds. For example, listed compounds are protected from internal modification while unlisted compounds are not. And it would appear that listing also favours fore-stress, in several ways. Firstly, I argued above that listing is a natural consequence of the semantic underspecification that goes with associative attribution, which itself favours fore-stress. Secondly, listing is linked to frequency in that high frequency encourages whole-word (i.e., list) access; and high frequency favours fore-stress (Plag et al. 2008; Bell and Plag 2012). Thirdly, the same authors show that in terms of orthographic behaviour, concatenated spelling (*girlfriend, girl-friend* vs. *girl friend*) is linked to high frequency, and thereby indirectly again to fore-stress and to listing. And fourth, syntactic (adjectival ascriptive) attribution is, as I showed in section 5.2.3, subject to sporadic lexicalisation: *black coffee, black-board, blackbird*. If we assume that in such cases, lexicalisation has been a diachronic process changing the status of such items from spontaneous formation to listed item, and in some cases, perhaps completing the process, from noun phrase to noun, then there is a further link between listing and possible fore-stress. We know that lexicalisation relates to frequency and to formal and semantic change (Hohenhaus 2005; Brinton and Traugott 2005); but this essentially diachronic phenomenon cannot be accounted for in terms of the present theory as long as that theory does not express a listing facility on the stratum preceding the syntax.

As I have noted before, failure to model a listing facility on stratum 2 of the lexicon has been a severe shortcoming of lexicalism, specifically of the theory of lexical morphology. Even without knowing how such a facility might be expressed in the theory, we know that it has a significant role to play in predicting and explaining various aspects of compound behaviour. Formal accounts can side-step this issue to some extent, as I have in this chapter, by using associativeness as some kind of proxy for (non-'lexicalised') listing, and by contrasting the behaviour of clearly listed items (*milk-leg, severe weather warning*) with the behaviour shown by items which are clearly not listed, such as *ethnographical conditioning lecture* and the *gay clergy book row priest*. But this does not cover the listing resulting from lexicalisation, noted above. As long as the framework fails to model that list itself and its integration into the formal derivational devices of the stratum, it has no systematic way of accounting for some crucial, yet often non-categorical features of compounds. But the account offered in this chapter at least predicts unpredictability on formal grounds, and in doing so it makes space available for probabilistic explanations.

References

Ackema, Peter. 1999. *Issues in morphosyntax*. Amsterdam: Benjamins.

Adams, Valerie. 1973. *An introduction to modern English word-formation*. Harlow: Longman.

Adams, Valerie. 2001. *Complex words in English*. Harlow: Longman.

Allen, Margaret R. 1978. *Morphological investigations*. PhD thesis. Storrs: University of Connecticut.

Allen, Margaret R. 1980. Semantic and phonological consequences of boundaries: A morphological analysis of compounds. In: Mark Aronoff and Marie Louise Kean (eds) *Juncture: A collection of original papers*. Saratoga: Anma Libri.

Allen, W. Sidney. 1973. *Accent and rhythm: Prosodic features in Latin and Greek*. Cambridge: Cambridge University Press.

Anderson, John M. 2004. On the grammatical status of names. *Language* 80: 435–74.

Anderson, Stephen R. 1982. Where's morphology? *Linguistic Inquiry* 13: 571–612.

Anshen, Frank and Mark Aronoff. 1981. Morphological productivity and phonological transparency. *Canadian Journal of Linguistics* 26: 63–72.

Arndt-Lappe, Sabine. 2014. Analogy in suffix rivalry: The case of English *-ity* and *-ness*. *English Language and Linguistics* 18: 497–548.

Aronoff, Mark. 1976. *Word formation in generative grammar*. Cambridge MA: MIT Press.

Aronoff, Mark and S. N. Sridhar. 1987. Morphological levels in English and Kannada. In: Edmund Gussmann (ed.) *Rules and the lexicon: Studies in word formation*. Lublin: Redakcja Wydawnictw Katolickiego Uniwersytetu Lubelskiego.

Baayen, Harald. 1993. On frequency, transparency and productivity. *Yearbook of Morphology 1993*: 181–298.

Baeskow, Heike. 2004. *Lexical properties of selected non-native morphemes of English*. Tübingen: Narr.

Baeskow, Heike. 2012. *-Ness* and *-ity*: Phonological exponents of *n* or meaningful nominalizers of different adjectival domains? *Journal of English Linguistics* 40: 6–40.

Baker, Mark C. 2003. *Lexical categories: Verbs, nouns, and adjectives.* Cambridge: Cambridge University Press.

Bauer, Laurie. 1978. *The grammar of nominal compounding with special reference to Danish, English and French.* Odense: Odense University Press.

Bauer, Laurie. 1990. Level disorder: the case of *-er* and *-or. Transactions of the Philological Society* 88: 97–110.

Bauer, Laurie. 1998. When is a sequence of two nouns a compound in English? *English Language and Linguistics* 2: 65–86.

Bauer, Laurie. 2004. Adjectives, compounds and words. *Worlds of words: A tribute to Arne Zettersten* (= *Nordic Journal of English Studies, Special Issue* 3.1: 7–22).

Bauer, Laurie. 2008. Dvandva. *Word Structure* 1: 1–20.

Bauer, Laurie, Rochelle Lieber and Ingo Plag. 2013. *The Oxford reference guide to English morphology.* Oxford: Oxford University Press.

Bell, Melanie and Ingo Plag. 2012. Informativeness is a determinant of compound stress in English. *Journal of Linguistics* 48: 485–520.

Bell, Melanie and Ingo Plag. 2013. Compound stress, informativity and analogy. *Word Structure* 6: 129–55.

Bermúdez-Otero, Ricardo. 2003. The acquisition of phonological opacity. In: J. Spenader, A. Eriksson and Östen Dahl (eds) *Variation within optimality theory: Proceedings of the Stockholm workshop on variation within optimality theory.* Stockholm: Department of Linguistics, University of Stockholm.

Bermúdez-Otero, Ricardo and April McMahon. 2006. English phonology and morphology. In: Bas Aarts and April McMahon (eds) *The handbook of English linguistics.* Oxford: Blackwell.

Bisetto, Antonietta and Sergio Scalise. 1999. Compounding: morphology and/or syntax? In: L. Mereu (ed.) *The boundaries of morphology and syntax.* Amsterdam: Benjamins.

Bloomfield, Leonard. 1933. *Language.* London: Allen and Unwin.

Boas, Hans C. 2010. The syntax–lexicon continuum in construction grammar: A case study of English communication verbs. *Belgian Journal of Linguistics* 24: 54–82.

Bolinger, Dwight. 1972. Accent is predictable (if you're a mind-reader). *Language* 48: 633–44.

Booij, Geert. 1985. Coordination reduction in complex words: A case for prosodic phonology. In: Harry van der Hulst and Norval Smith (eds) *Advances in nonlinear phonology.* Dordrecht: Foris.

Booij, Geert. 1994. Lexical phonology: A review. In: Richard Wiese (ed.) *Recent developments in lexical phonology.* Düsseldorf: Heinrich-Heine-Universität.

Booij, Geert. 1996. Inherent versus contextual inflection and the split morphology hypothesis. *Yearbook of Morphology 1995*: 1–16.

Booij, Geert. 1999. The role of the prosodic word in phonotactic generalisations. In: T. Alan Hall and Ursula Kleinhenz (eds) *Studies on the phonological word.* Amsterdam: Benjamins.

Booij, Geert. 2009. Phrasal names: A constructionist analysis. In: Barbara Schlücker and Matthias Hüning (eds) *Words and phrases: Nominal expressions of naming and description* (= *Word Structure* 2.2: 219–40). Edinburgh: Edinburgh University Press.

Booij, Geert and Jerzy Rubach. 1987. Postcyclic vs. postlexical rules in lexical phonology. *Linguistic Inquiry* 18: 1–44.

Borowsky, Toni. 1990. *Topics in the lexical phonology of English*. New York: Garland.

Botha, Rudolph P. 1983. *Morphological mechanisms*. Oxford: Pergamon Press.

Bouchard, Denis. 2002. *Adjectives, number and interfaces: Why languages vary*. London: Elsevier.

Bresnan, Joan and Sam Mchombo. 1995. The Lexical Integrity Principle: Evidence from Bantu. *Natural Language and Linguistic Theory* 13: 181–254.

Brinton, Laurel J. and Elizabeth Closs Traugott. 2005. *Lexicalization and language change*. Cambridge: Cambridge University Press.

Broccias, Cristiano. 2012. The syntax–lexicon continuum. In: Terttu Nevalainen and Elizabeth Closs Traugott (eds) *The Oxford handbook of the history of English*. Oxford: Oxford University Press.

Burton-Roberts, Noel. 2011. *Analysing sentences*. 3rd edn. London: Longman.

Burzio, Luigi. 1994. *Principles of English stress*. Cambridge: Cambridge University Press.

Carstairs-McCarthy, Andrew. 2002. *An introduction to English morphology: Words and their structure*. Edinburgh: Edinburgh University Press.

Carstairs-McCarthy, Andrew. 2005. Phrases inside compounds: A puzzle for lexicon-free morphology. *SKASE Journal of Theoretical Linguistics* 2.3: 34–42.

Chomsky, Noam. 1965. *Aspects of the theory of syntax*. Cambridge MA: MIT Press.

Chomsky, Noam. 1970. Remarks on nominalization. In: Roderick A. Jacobs and Peter S. Rosenbaum (eds) *Readings in English transformational grammar*. Waltham: Ginn.

Chomsky, Noam and Morris Halle. 1968. *The sound pattern of English*. New York: Harper and Row.

Collie, Sarah. 2008. English stress preservation: The case for 'fake cyclicity'. *English Language and Linguistics* 12: 505–32.

Croft, William. 2001. *Radical construction grammar: Syntactic theory in typological perspective*. Oxford: Oxford University Press.

Di Sciullo, Anna Maria and Edwin Williams. 1987. *On the definition of word*. Cambridge MA: MIT Press.

Dogil, Grzegorz. 1979. *Autosegmental account of phonological emphasis*. Edmonton: Linguistic Research.

Downing, Pamela. 1977. On the creation and use of English compounds. *Language* 53: 810–43.

Faiß, Klaus. 1978. *Verdunkelte Compounds im Englischen: Ein Beitrag zur Theorie und Praxis der Wortbildung*. Tübingen: Narr.

Faiß, Klaus. 1981. Compound, pseudo-compound and syntactic group especially in English. In: Peter Kunsmann and Ortwin Kuhn (eds) *Weltsprache Englisch in Forschung und Lehre: Festschrift für Kurt Wächtler*. Berlin: Schmidt.

Fanselow, Gisbert. 1981. *Zur Syntax und Semantik der Nominalkomposition: Ein Versuch praktischer Anwendung der Montague-Grammatik auf die Wortbildung im Deutschen*. Tübingen: Niemeyer.

Ferris, Connor. 1993. *The meaning of syntax: A study in the adjectives of English*. London: Longman.

Frauenfelder, Uli and Robert Schreuder. 1992. Constraining psycholinguistic models of morphological processing and representation: The role of productivity. *Yearbook of Morphology 1991*: 165–83.

Fudge, Erik. 1984. *English word-stress*. London: Allen and Unwin.

Giegerich, Heinz J. 1992. *English phonology: An introduction*. Cambridge: Cambridge University Press.

Giegerich, Heinz J. 1999. *Lexical strata in English: Morphological causes, phonological effects*. Cambridge: Cambridge University Press.

Giegerich, Heinz J. 2001. Synonymy blocking and the Elsewhere Condition: Lexical morphology and the speaker. *Transactions of the Philological Society* 99: 65–98.

Giegerich, Heinz J. 2004. Compound or phrase? English noun-plus-noun constructions and the stress criterion. *English Language and Linguistics* 8: 1–24.

Giegerich, Heinz J. 2005a. Associative adjectives in English and the lexicon–syntax interface. *Journal of Linguistics* 41: 571–91.

Giegerich, Heinz J. 2005b. Lexicalism and modular overlap in English. *SKASE Journal of Theoretical Linguistics* 2.2: 43–62.

Giegerich, Heinz J. 2006. Attribution in English and the distinction between phrases and compounds. In: Petr Rösel (ed.) *English in space and time – Englisch in Raum und Zeit: Forschungsbericht zu Ehren von Klaus Faiß*. Trier: Wissenschaftlicher Verlag Trier.

Giegerich, Heinz J. 2009a. Compounding and lexicalism. In: Rochelle Lieber and Pavol Štekauer (eds) *The Oxford handbook of compounding*. Oxford: Oxford University Press.

Giegerich, Heinz J. 2009b. The English compound stress myth. *Word Structure* 2: 1–17.

Giegerich, Heinz J. 2012. Phrasal fore-stress in English. In: Eugeniusz Cyran, Henryk Cardela and Bogdan Szymanek (eds) *Sound structure and sense: Studies in memory of Edmund Gussmann*. Lublin: Wydawnictwo KUL.

Goldberg, Adele. 2006. *Constructions at work: The nature of generalisation in language*. Oxford: Oxford University Press.

Götz, Dieter. 1971. *Studien zu den verdunkelten Komposita im Englischen*. Nürnberg: H. Carl.

Grant, William and James Main Dixon. 1921. *Manual of Modern Scots*. London: Cambridge University Press.

Grimshaw, Jane. 1992. *Argument structure*. Cambridge MA: MIT Press.

Hall, T. Alan. 1999. The phonological word: A review. In: T. Alan Hall and Ursula Kleinhenz (eds) *Studies on the phonological word*. Amsterdam: Benjamins.

Halle, Morris. 1973. Prolegomena to a theory of word formation. *Linguistic Inquiry* 4: 3–16.

Halle, Morris and S. Jay Keyser. 1971. *English stress: Its form, its growth, and its role in verse*. New York: Harper and Row.

Halle, Morris and K. P. Mohanan. 1985. Segmental phonology of modern English. *Linguistic Inquiry* 16: 57–116.

Halle, Morris and Jean-Roger Vergnaud. 1987. *An essay on stress*. Cambridge MA: MIT Press.

Halliday, Michael A. K. 1967. *Intonation and grammar in British English*. The Hague: Mouton.

Haspelmath, Martin. 2011. The indeterminacy of word segmentation and the nature of morphology and syntax. *Folia Linguistica* 45: 31–80.

Hay, Jennifer. 2002. From speech perception to morphology: Affix ordering revisited. *Language* 78: 527–55.

Hay, Jennifer. 2003. *Causes and consequences of word structure*. Abingdon: Taylor and Francis.

Hayes, Bruce. 1982. Extrametricality and English stress. *Linguistic Inquiry* 13: 227–76.

Hohenhaus, Peter. 2005. Lexicalization and institutionalization. In: Pavol Štekauer and Rochelle Lieber (eds) *Handbook of word-formation*. Berlin: Springer.

Hornstein, Norbert and David Lightfoot. 1981. *Explanation in linguistics: The logical problem of language acquisition*. London: Longman.

Hyman, Larry. 1977. On the nature of linguistic stress. In: Larry Hyman (ed.) *Studies in stress and accent*. Los Angeles: Department of Linguistics, University of Southern California.

Jackendoff, Ray. 1997. *The architecture of the language faculty*. Cambridge MA: MIT Press.

Jespersen, Otto. 1924. *The philosophy of grammar*. London: Allen and Unwin; New York: Holt.

Jespersen, Otto. 1942. *A Modern English grammar on historical principles. Part VI: Morphology*. London: Allen and Unwin; Copenhagen: Munksgaard.

Jones, Charles. 1997. Phonology. In: Charles Jones (ed.) *The Edinburgh history of the Scots language*. Edinburgh: Edinburgh University Press.

Kastovsky, Dieter. 1982. *Wortbildung und Semantik*. Düsseldorf: Francke.

Katz, Jerrold J. and Paul M. Postal. 1964. *An integrated theory of linguistic descriptions*. Cambridge MA: MIT Press.

Kingdon, Roger. 1958. *The groundwork of English stress*. London: Longman.

Kiparsky, Paul. 1979. Metrical structure assignment is cyclic. *Linguistic Inquiry* 10: 421–41.

Kiparsky, Paul. 1982. Lexical morphology and phonology. In: Linguistic Society of Korea (eds) *Linguistics in the morning calm: Selected papers from SICOL-1981*. Seoul: Hanshin.

Kiparsky, Paul. 1985. Some consequences of lexical phonology. *Phonology Yearbook* 2: 85–138.

Kiparsky, Paul. 2000. Opacity and cyclicity. *Linguistic Review* 17: 351–65.

Koshiishi, Tetsuya. 2002. Collateral adjectives, Latinate vocabulary, and English morphology. *Studia Anglica Posnaniensia* 37: 49–88.

Koshiishi, Tetsuya. 2011. *Collateral adjectives and related issues.* Berne: Lang.

Kösling, Kristina and Ingo Plag. 2009. Does branching direction determine prominence assignment? An empirical investigation of triconstituent compounds in English. *Corpus Linguistics and Linguistic Theory* 5: 205–43.

Koziol, Herbert. 1937. *Handbuch der englischen Wortbildungslehre.* Heidelberg: Carl Winter's Universitätsbuchhandlung.

Kvam, Anders Martin. 1990. Three-part noun combinations in English: Composition – meaning – stress. *English Studies* 71: 152–60.

Ladd, D. Robert. 1980. *The structure of intonational meaning: Evidence from English.* Bloomington: Indiana University Press.

Ladd, D. Robert. 1984. English compound stress. In: Dafydd Gibbon and Helmut Richter (eds) *Intonation, accent, and rhythm.* Berlin: de Gruyter.

Laks, Lior. 2013. Passive formation in Palestinian and Standard Arabic: Lexical vs. syntactic operations. *Word Structure* 6: 156–80.

Langacker, Ronald W. 1987. *Foundations of cognitive grammar. Volume 1: Theoretical prerequisites.* Stanford: Stanford University Press.

Langacker, Ronald W. 1991. *Foundations of cognitive grammar. Volume 2: Descriptive applications.* Stanford: Stanford University Press.

Lapointe, Steven G. 1980. *A theory of grammatical agreement.* PhD dissertation. Amherst: University of Massachusetts.

Lees, Robert. 1963. *The grammar of English nominalizations.* Bloomington: Indiana University.

Leitzke, Eva. 1989. *(De)nominale Adjektive im heutigen Englisch: Untersuchungen zur Morphologie, Syntax, Semantik und Pragmatik von Adjektiv-Nomen-Kombinationen der Typen* atomic energy *and* criminal lawyer. Tübingen: Niemeyer.

Levi, Judith N. 1978. *The syntax and semantics of complex nominals.* New York: Academic Press.

Liberman, Mark and Alan Prince. 1977. On stress and linguistic rhythm. *Linguistic Inquiry* 8: 249–336.

Liberman, Mark and Richard Sproat. 1992. The stress and structure of modified noun phrases in English. In: Ivan A. Sag and Anna Scabolcsi (eds) *Lexical matters.* Stanford: Center for the Study of Language and Information.

Lieber, Rochelle. 1983. Argument linking and compounds in English. *Linguistic Inquiry* 14: 251–85.

Lieber, Rochelle. 1992. *Deconstructing morphology.* Chicago: University of Chicago Press.

Lipka, Leonhard. 1994. Lexicalization and institutionalization. In: R. E. Asher (ed.) *The encyclopedia of language and linguistics.* Oxford: Pergamon Press.

Lipka, Leonhard, Susanne Handl and Wolfgang Falkner. 2004. Lexicalization and institutionalization: The state of the art in 2004. *SKASE Journal of Theoretical Linguistics* 1: 2–18.

Marchand, Hans. 1969. *The categories and types of present-day English word-formation: A synchronic-diachronic approach.* 2nd edn. Munich: Beck.

Mårdh, Ingrid. 1980. *Headlinese: On the grammar of English front page headlines.* Malmö: Liberläromedel/Gleerup.

McMahon, April. 1990. Vowel shift, free rides and strict cyclicity. *Lingua* 80: 197–225.

McMahon, April. 2000. *Lexical phonology and the history of English.* Cambridge: Cambridge University Press.

Mohanan, K. P. 1986. *The theory of lexical phonology.* Dordrecht: Reidel.

Newman, Paul. 1972. Syllable weight as a phonological variable. *Studies in African Linguistics* 3: 301–24.

Olsen, Susan. 2000. Compounding and stress in English: A closer look at the boundary between morphology and syntax. *Linguistische Berichte* 181: 55–69.

Olsen, Susan. 2001. Copulative compounds: A closer look at the distinction between morphology and syntax. *Yearbook of Morphology 2000*: 279–320.

Payne, John and Rodney Huddleston. 2002. Nouns and noun phrases. In: Rodney Huddleston and Geoffrey K. Pullum, *The Cambridge grammar of the English language.* Cambridge: Cambridge University Press.

Pinker, Steven. 1999. *Words and rules: The ingredients of language.* New York: Basic Books.

Plag, Ingo. 1999. *Morphological productivity: Structural constraints in English derivation.* Berlin: Mouton de Gruyter.

Plag, Ingo. 2003. *Word-formation in English.* Cambridge: Cambridge University Press.

Plag, Ingo. 2004. Syntactic category information and the semantics of derivational morphological rules. *Folia Linguistica* 38: 193–225.

Plag, Ingo. 2006. The variability of compound stress in English: Structural, semantic and analogical factors. *English Language and Linguistics* 10: 143–72.

Plag, Ingo. 2010. Compound stress assignment by analogy: The constituent family bias. *Zeitschrift für Sprachwissenschaft* 29: 243–82.

Plag, Ingo, Gero Kunter, Sabine Lappe and Maria Braun. 2008. The role of semantics, argument structure, and lexicalization in compound stress assignment in English. *Language* 84: 760–94.

Poser, William. 1992. Blocking of phrasal constructions by lexical items. In: Ivan A. Sag and Anna Scabolcsi (eds) *Lexical matters.* Stanford: Center for the Study of Language and Information.

Price, Rebecca. 2014. *Headlines, compounds and lexicalism.* MA dissertation. Edinburgh: University of Edinburgh.

Pullum, Geoffrey K. and Rodney Huddleston. 2002. Adjectives and adverbs. In: Rodney Huddleston and Geoffrey K. Pullum, *The Cambridge grammar of the English language.* Cambridge: Cambridge University Press.

Pustejovsky, James. 1995. *The generative lexicon*. Cambridge MA: MIT Press.

Quirk, Randolph, Sidney Greenbaum, Geoffrey Leech and Jan Svartvik. 1985. *A comprehensive grammar of the English language*. London: Longman.

Radford, Andrew. 1988. *Transformational grammar*. Cambridge: Cambridge University Press.

Rauh, Gisa. 2010. *Syntactic categories: Their identification and description in linguistic theories*. Oxford: Oxford University Press.

Riddle, Elizabeth M. 1985. A historical perspective on the productivity of the suffixes *-ness* and *-ity*. In: Jacek Fisiak (ed.) *Historical semantics, historical word-formation*. Berlin: Mouton.

Rischel, Jørgen. 1972. Compound stress in Danish without a cycle. *Annual Report of the Institute of Phonetics, University of Copenhagen* 6: 211–18.

Scalise, Sergio. 1984. *Generative morphology*. Dordrecht: Foris.

Scalise, Sergio and Emiliano Guevara. 2005. The lexicalist approach to word-formation. In: Pavol Štekauer and Rochelle Lieber (eds) *Handbook of word-formation*. Dordrecht: Springer.

Schlücker, Barbara and Matthias Hüning. 2009. Introduction. In: Barbara Schlücker and Matthias Hüning (eds) *Words and phrases: Nominal expressions of naming and description* (= *Word Structure* 2.2: 149–54). Edinburgh: Edinburgh University Press.

Schmerling, Susan. 1971. A stress mess. *Studies in the Linguistic Sciences* 1: 52–66.

Schmerling, Susan. 1976. *Aspects of English sentence stress*. Austin: University of Texas Press.

Selkirk, Elisabeth O. 1980. The role of prosodic categories in English word stress. *Linguistic Inquiry* 11: 563–605.

Selkirk, Elisabeth O. 1982. *The syntax of words*. Cambridge MA: MIT Press.

Shore, Todd. 2010. Making sense of adjectives: Association vs. ascription in a family-resemblance model of semantic inheritance. *SKASE Journal of Theoretical Linguistics* 7.3: 2–17.

Siegel, Dorothy. 1979. *Topics in English morphology*. New York: Garland.

Siegel, Muffy. 1980. *Capturing the adjective*. New York: Garland.

Spencer, Andrew. 1988. Bracketing paradoxes and the English lexicon. *Language* 64: 663–82.

Spencer, Andrew. 1991. *Morphological theory*. Oxford: Blackwell.

Sproat, Richard. 1985. *On deriving the lexicon*. Cambridge MA: MIT Working Papers in Linguistics.

Sproat, Richard. 1994. English noun-phrase accent prediction for text-to-speech. *Computer Speech and Language* 8: 79–94.

Stirling, Lesley and Rodney Huddleston. 2002. Deixis and anaphora. In: Rodney Huddleston and Geoffrey K. Pullum, *The Cambridge grammar of the English language*. Cambridge: Cambridge University Press.

Stump, Gregory. 2010. The derivation of compound ordinal numerals: Implications for morphological theory. *Word Structure* 3: 205–33.

Sweet, Henry. 1900. *A new English grammar, logical and historical.* Oxford: Clarendon Press.

Szpyra, Jolanta. 1989. *The morphology–phonology interface: Cycles, levels and words.* London: Routledge.

ten Hacken, Pius. 2013. Semiproductivity and the place of word formation in grammar. In: Pius ten Hacken and Claire Thomas (eds) *The semantics of word formation and lexicalization.* Edinburgh: Edinburgh University Press.

ten Hacken, Pius and Claire Thomas. 2013. Word formation, meaning and lexicalization. In: Pius ten Hacken and Claire Thomas (eds) *The semantics of word formation and lexicalization.* Edinburgh: Edinburgh University Press.

Thomas, Claire. 2013. Lexicalization in generative morphology and conceptual structure. In: Pius ten Hacken and Claire Thomas (eds) *The semantics of word formation and lexicalization.* Edinburgh: Edinburgh University Press.

Trager, George L. and Henry L. Smith. 1951. *An outline of English structure.* Norman: Battenburg Press.

van Santen, Ariane. 1986. Synthetic compounds: Syntax or semantics? *Linguistics* 24: 645–60.

Warren, Beatrice. 1884. *Classifying adjectives.* Gothenburg: Acta Universitatis Gothoburgensis.

Wiese, Richard. 1996a. Phrasal compounds and the theory of word syntax. *Linguistic Inquiry* 27: 183–93.

Wiese, Richard. 1996b. *The phonology of German.* Oxford: Clarendon Press.

Williams, Edwin. 1981. On the notions *lexically related* and *head of a word. Linguistic Inquiry* 12: 245–74.

Zwicky, Arnold. 1986. Forestress and afterstress. *Ohio State University Working Papers in Linguistics* 32: 46–62.

Author index

Subject index

Page numbers in **bold** indicate major coverage.